Study Guide

to accompany

Kishlansky • Geary • O'Brien

CIVILIZATION IN THE WEST

Sixth Edition
Volume Two

Paul Brasil

Blue Mountain Community College

PEARSON
Longman

New York Boston San Francisco
London Toronto Sydney Tokyo Singapore Madrid
Mexico City Munich Paris Cape Town Hong Kong Montreal

Study Guide, Volume II to accompany *Civilization in the West, 6/e*

ISBN: 0-321-31696-7

1 2 3 4 5 6 7 8 9 10-OPM-08 07 06 05

CONTENTS

Introduction

The *Study Guide* is keyed to help the student understand the comparative and connective aspects of the text. Rather than focus on rote memorization of data, the *Study Guide* emphasizes recognition of major themes and interpretation of connective links among civilizations. Each chapter within the text is covered in the *Study Guide* so that the student proceeds from the specific data to the important summary themes and comparative conclusions.

Most chapters of the *Study Guide* include the following elements:

• An outline demonstrating the organization of each chapter in the text and the major historical points covered;

• A timeline asking the student to organize major events in each chapter chronologically;

• A list of important terms, people, and events to be defined;

• A map exercise establishing the geopolitical structure of the chapter;

• A series of short questions entitled "Making Connections" seeking to establish students' familiarity with larger blocks of information connecting the items found in "Terms, People, Events;"

• Two broad essays stressing the major interpretive points of each chapter and asking students to make significant comparisons and contrasts among historical periods;

• A self-test of factual information featuring multiple-choice questions covering both specific data and general interpretations. A selection of these questions is taken directly from the Test Bank for *Civilization in the West*.

How should you use the *Study Guide*? Read the text chapter first. The *Study Guide* was not intended to replace the text, simply to supplement it. After your first reading, look at the outline in the Study Guide. The outline should help you to organize the elements of the chapter and point out important concepts. Arrange the chapter chronologically by filling out the timeline. It may be helpful to compare the timeline for the chapter on which you are working with those of other chapters to gain a comparative view of political, social, and economic events. Once the organization of the chapter and its chronological framework is clear to you, move on to the "Terms, People, Events." These specific points of information can best be handled by writing out definitions for each—perhaps in your notebook. You may discover that these terms can be supplemented by items covered in lecture. "Making Connections" asks you to take the major points in the outline and put them together in short essay form. The purpose of putting blocks of information together is to make certain that you understand relationships between important people and events. The last activity in the Study Guide—"Putting Larger Concepts Together"— asks you to make broad generalizations about the major themes of each chapter and, occasionally, to compare the ideas explored in one chapter with material from earlier chapters. These may be more difficult to accomplish, but they check your ability to understand the comparative developments in European history. Essays covered in "Putting Larger Concepts Together" could be used as a focus for in-class discussion or possibly as examination questions. Remember, the *Study Guide* is coordinated with the Test Bank.

No study guide can guarantee a good grade. The text and the *Study Guide* represent only one component of the course. Individual instructors may vary in their approaches to the course. Lectures may incorporate materials not included in the text or differ dramatically in interpretation. Instructors may opt not to use the *Test Bank* in order to offer questions that more closely parallel their own treatment of the course. In any case, the *Study Guide* will strengthen your understanding of *Civilization in the West* and enable you to understand the broad patterns of change in European history.

The West to 1600

The Agricultural Revolution of the Neolithic Age, beginning perhaps as early as 10,000 B.C.E., led to the development of sedentary agricultural communities in the mountain foothills of the Near East. Migration from the foothills to the nearby Tigris-Euphrates and Nile River valleys resulted in the formation of the two first civilizations of the West—Egypt and Mesopotamia. Each was, in its own way, distinctive, but both of the earliest Western civilizations shared certain basic traits—urbanization, systems of writing, militarization, social stratification, economic specialization, religion and ritual, and sophisticated political systems leading to the development of empires. Neither of these ancient civilizations was immune to invasion and collapse. Often nomadic peoples who existed on the borders of civilizations were the catalysts for political chaos within the empires. There was a constant cycle of political consolidation, stagnation, decline, and dynastic collapse.

About a millennium after the advent of civilizations in Egypt and Mesopotamia, a similarly complex society began to develop on the Cyclades, Crete, the coast of Asia Minor, and the mainland of Greece. After a temporary period of cultural decline between 1100 and 800 B.C.E., Greek civilization emerged as a politically decentralized collection of city-states bound together by a shared language and culture. Unlike either Egypt or the Mesopotamian cultures, Greek civilization experienced only a brief period of imperial expansion under Alexander the Great of Macedonia. Greek civilization was particularly important to the later development of the West because of the intellectual foundations established by such important philosophers as Plato and Aristotle. Greek rationalism became the underpinning for the religious and philosophical systems of subsequent Western civilization.

Beginning around 1000 B.C.E., sedentary agricultural communities began to develop in the Italian peninsula. Like Greece, early Italian societies were organized as city-states. Etruscan civilization, located in northern Italy, was briefly able to form a confederation of cities. The city-state of Rome, at one time ruled by Etruscan kings, declared its independence from the Etruscan confederation in the sixth century B.C.E. and came to dominate first the Italian peninsula and then the entire Mediterranean basin. The Roman republic drew its strength from its legions composed of free citizens. These armies crushed first the other city-states of the Italian peninsula, then Carthage, Rome's chief rival for dominance in the western Mediterranean. By the second century B.C.E., Greek civilization fell under Rome's aegis. The conquest of vast territories created both economic and political problems that overwhelmed the republic. By the first century C.E., Rome's government was transformed into a politically centralized empire. With a major reform at the end of the third century C.E., the republic survived in the West until 476. The eastern Roman world flourished until 1453 as the Byzantine Empire. Contemporary with the creation of the Roman Empire was the emergence of Christianity. From its origins in Palestine in the first century C.E., Christianity expanded throughout the empire. In the fourth century C.E., the Emperor Constantine granted official sanction to the still new religion.

In the fifth century C.E., the western half of the Roman Empire came under increasing pressure from Germanic invaders. As the central government began to lose control over distant provinces, Germanic kings with the cooperation of regional Roman elites formed more localized kingdoms. Significant to the recognition of these Germanic rulers were the bishops of the Christian Church, who often took over the local functions of government. The most successful of the Germanic groups in western Europe was the Franks. Under the Merovingian and Carolingian dynasties, the Franks carved out a kingdom that included much of modern-day France and Germany. In recognition of the success of Charlemagne, the most successful of the Carolingian rulers, the pope recognized the Frankish king as emperor in 800. The restoration of the empire in the person of the Carolingian monarch represented more the idea of a united Christendom than the physical restoration of the empire. Despite Charlemagne's many accomplishments, the most powerful of the Carolingians lacked a well-developed central administration capable of governing his vast territories. Under the pressure of renewed invasions beginning shortly after Charlemagne's death in 814, the Carolingian empire collapsed.

The Europe that emerged after the disintegration of the Carolingian empire consisted of much more localized political units. In those areas that had once been part of the Roman Empire, feudalism provided a basis for political organization. Feudal monarchies were established in England, France, and southern Italy. In those areas of Germany that had always been outside the boundaries of the Roman Empire, the principles of Germanic government derived from the Carolingians continued to survive. Slowly the kingdom of the Germans was organized under the direction of a titular leader, who continued to be called emperor. As with the Carolingian empire, the new Holy Roman Empire lacked the administrative centralization to create a unified state and remained a collection of small principalities, bishoprics, private estates, and imperial cities. In many ways the most direct heir of the ancient imperial tradition was the Christian Church. The bishops of Rome created a universal government recognized in all the other political units of Europe by the twelfth century. In northern Italy and within the lands bordering the Holy Roman Empire and the states of western Europe, independent city-states—some the remnants of ancient cities, others new foundations—provided the basis for a commercial renaissance.

Perhaps more important than the political resuscitation of the West was the economic rebirth that occurred during the Middle Ages. It was in the city-states of Italy that the cultural phenomenon called the Renaissance occurred. The prosperity and independence of the Italian cities promoted a rebirth of classical learning and a remarkable period of artistic creativity.

The renewed interest in classical studies also prompted closer examination of Christian documents, particularly the Bible. Christian humanists began the process of criticizing the foundations of the Catholic Church of Europe. One of those engaged in biblical studies was a German Augustinian monk named Martin Luther. His examination of the New Testament led him to question basic Catholic orthodoxy concerning the remission of sin, the role of the clergy, the doctrine of Grace, and the authority of the pope. Luther's inability to gain satisfactory reforms within the Church touched off the Protestant Reformation in the early sixteenth century. Theological differences between Catholics and Protestants destroyed the unity of Christendom. Protestants could not maintain theological unity among themselves. By the sixteenth century, there were no purely religious questions. Divisions within the Church became political rifts that widened into open war. Religious orthodoxy became an issue of the state.

CHAPTER 14

Europe at War, 1555-1648

OUTLINE

I. The Massacre of the Innocents

War was a common feature of European society even before the mid-sixteenth century. After 1550, warfare spread throughout the European continent. Violence linked together dynastic ambition, social rebellion, and sectarian hatred.

II. The Crises of the Western States

  A. Introduction

One king and one faith was the organizing principle for the monarchies of western Europe. The Protestant Reformation destroyed the easy unanimity of political power and religious faith. As European populations were divided in religious belief, internal disruption of the state and society was inevitable. Only the total victory of Catholics or a single variety of Protestantism could restore the solidarity of the state and society. As rulers choose the religion of their state, religious minorities were forced to uproot and migrate. The resulting bitterness and chaos produced a century of civil wars.

  B. The French Wars of Religion

Protestantism was exported to France from Calvin's Geneva. By 1560 Calvinism had gained a foothold in France, particularly within the provincial towns. At the same time, the death of the reigning French monarch Henry II, left his fifteen-year-old son and his widowed queen, Catherine de Medicis, in control of the royal administration. The weakened central government permitted the creation of a powerful political faction within the French aristocracy. The Catholic Guise family allied itself with the royal family and dominated the offices of state and of the Catholic Church in France. The Guises were intent on the destruction of Protestant nobles who represented a possible opposition. Their situation became less secure when Francis II died, leaving his younger brother, Charles IX, on the throne. Sensing the weakness of the Guise position, Protestant nobles led by the Bourbon family and Henry of Navarre raised armies and initiated a civil war in 1562. Neither side was able to gain a decisive advantage. The Protestants were reduced to defending cities in their control, largely in southern France. Catherine de Medicis unsuccessfully sought a truce that would guarantee the position of her remaining sons. An attempted compromise that would permit Protestantism among the nobility was undone when the head of the Guise family was assassinated. A second diplomatic effort was initiated in 1570. Henry of Navarre was offered the hand of Charles IX's sister with the wedding to take place in Paris. The proposed marriage proved to be a deception intended to lure Protestant leaders to the capital city where they could be slaughtered by the Guise retainers. The result was the Saint Bartholomew's Day Massacre of 1572. Many Protestants were murdered in the streets, but the leaders escaped.

C. One King, Two Faiths

The collusion of Catherine de Medicis in the Saint Bartholomew's Day Massacre allowed Henry of Navarre and the Huguenots (as French Protestants were called) to launch an attack on the monarchy itself. Some moderate Catholic nobles, appalled by the bloodshed in Paris, joined forces with the Huguenots. Conservative Catholics responded by forming the Catholic League. The League, still led by the Guise family, was even willing to alter the succession in order to avoid any compromise with the Protestants. The monarchy seemed on the verge of losing its authority to one or another of the parties. King Henry III ordered the assassination of the leading members of the Guise family and attempted to gain a treaty with Henry Bourbon and the Huguenots. The sad chronicle of political duplicity and murder reached its climax with the assassination of the king in 1589. The sole successor to the Valois throne was Henry Bourbon, king of Navarre and leader of the Huguenots. In order to make his claim acceptable, Henry IV renounced Protestantism and converted to Catholicism. Such a diplomatic conversion, however much it may have lacked in sincerity, allowed Henry to claim the support of the papacy and the moderate Catholics. Resistance to the monarchy collapsed. In 1589, Henry made the settlement as palatable as possible to the Huguenots by offering them limited toleration in the Edict of Nantes. The passions of religious division were not entirely calmed. An assassin murdered Henry IV in 1610.

D. The World of Philip II

Spain under King Philip II was the most powerful nation in sixteenth-century Europe. His domain included Naples, Milan, the Netherlands, Portugal, and the colonies of the New World. Philip exercised a personal supervision over the affairs of his far-flung empire. Philip also presented himself as the protector of Catholicism and the scourge of Protestantism. Briefly married to Mary I, the Catholic queen of England, Philip hoped to retain England for Catholicism and as a Spanish ally. When Mary's successor, Elizabeth I, returned England to the Protestant Anglican Church and allowed English pirates to attack Spanish shipping, Philip amassed a great armada to attempt an amphibious assault on England. The Armada was largely destroyed by weather and English ships in 1588.

E. The Burgundian Inheritance

Philip's attempts to secure Catholic orthodoxy were particularly problematic in the Low Countries. The source of conflict was the rapid dissemination of Calvinism in the tolerant communities of the Low Countries and Philip's attempts to enforce the decrees of the Council of Trent. Both the local nobility and the town governments refused to implement the repressive measures of Philip's decrees.

F. The Revolt of the Netherlands

A Calvinist assault on Catholic churches initiated violence. The Spanish government viewed the iconoclasm as open rebellion with the tacit approval of the local nobility. Philip dispatched an army under the command of the Duke of Alba to restore order and orthodoxy. Alba imposed a martial reign of terror. Protestant nobles and suspected revolutionaries were executed under the authority of the military tribunal, the Council of Blood. In the short term, brutal suppression of Protestantism was effective. The Protestant movement was supported by those who resented not only the presence of the Spanish army, but also the taxation required to support it. In 1572 a full-scale civil war between the Spanish regents and Protestants ensued. Prince William of Orange led the Protestant movement, centered in the provinces of Holland and Zeeland. Alba's failure led to his removal from command, but undisciplined Spanish troops continued to loot the towns of the southern Low Countries. Brussels, Ghent, and Antwerp were sacked. The unrestrained violence of the Spanish army so discredited the Spanish presence in the Netherlands that Philip II granted autonomy in the Pacification of Ghent of 1576. What remained was a divided territory. Five provinces agreed to remain Catholic and recognize the authority of the Spanish monarch. The remainder declared their independence. Despite continual military efforts to bring the northern provinces back under the aegis of the Spanish government, Holland remained independent. The war was economically ruinous for all involved.

III.   The Struggles in Eastern Europe

A. Introduction

Dynastic struggles more than religious discord troubled the states of eastern Europe.

B. Kings and Diets in Poland

In 1572 Sigismund II, the last of the Jagiellons, died. In the absence of an heir, the Polish nobility elected the royal successors from available nobility elsewhere in Europe. In return for aristocratic favor, successful candidates conceded constitutional and religious rights to the nobility. The Polish Diet, a representative body of nobles, gained many powers, including the right to establish a policy of religious toleration. Throughout the sixteenth century, Poland-Lithuania remained militarily and economically strong. In 1587 Sigismund III, also heir to the Swedish crown, was elected king in Poland-Lithuania. While he accepted the principle of religious toleration, he acted to strengthen Roman Catholicism. Poland resolutely refused to support Sigismund's attempts to enforce his claims in Sweden.

C. Muscovy's Time of Troubles

Following the death of Ivan IV, the Terrible, the principality of Muscovy began to disintegrate. With no capable heir and without the support of the Muscovite aristocracy, the central government disintegrated. After 1601 numerous claimants to the throne battled with one another for superiority in the period referred to as the Time of Troubles. Poland-Lithuania sought to capitalize on the problems within Muscovy and to retake lands lost in the past. The Polish monarch, Sigismund III, turned from abortive campaigns in Sweden to an assault on Muscovy. When a plan to support one of the Muscovite claimants to the throne failed, Sigismund took Moscow and had himself proclaimed tsar in 1610. Sigismund III's reign as tsar of Muscovy was short-lived. In 1613 the Russian boyars united against a foreign enemy and elevated Michael Romanov to the office of tsar. Romanov was able to arrange for a peace with Poland in exchange for territorial concessions.

D. The Rise of Sweden

Sweden had been part of a Danish confederation until the rebellion of Gustav I Vasa in 1523. Thereafter Gustav ruled an independent Sweden in tandem with the Swedish aristocracy, who voiced their concerns through the Rad. Under Gustav, Sweden launched an aggressive foreign policy aimed at dominating the Baltic Sea regions. With the failure of the Teutonic Knights in Livonia, Sweden gained a foothold in Livonia on the Gulf of Finland through the fortification of sea ports on the Livonian coast. Sweden was soon drawn into conflict with Poland and Denmark over control of Baltic trade. Sigismund III of Poland had a claim to the Swedish throne. The Swedish aristocracy rebuffed Sigismund's attempts to secure both crowns and elected Charles IX in 1604. The election provoked conflict with Poland, but gave the Swedes an opportunity to extend their control over Livonia. Their primary objective was the port of Riga, a major center of eastern trade. Although the Swedish navy enjoyed success, the Poles destroyed their land forces. Only the Polish invasion of Muscovy saved the Swedes from loss of Livonia. Just as the Swedes were involved in the conflict with Poland, the king of Denmark, Christian IV, attempted to renew Danish claims to sovereignty in Sweden. In order to avoid a war on two fronts, the Swedes gave away nearly all of their trade advantages in the Baltic to Denmark in 1613. King Gustavus Adolphus (1611- 1632) succeeded Charles IX in the midst of the northern conflicts. With the invaluable support of the English and the Dutch—both of whom had trade interests in the Baltic—Gustavus Adolphus led the Swedes to military victory in the north. Renewed war with Poland ended the claims of Sigismund III to the Swedish throne and garnered the port of Riga. Muscovy surrendered its territories in the Gulf of Finland in return for Swedish support against the Poles. By 1619, Sweden was firmly in control of the eastern Baltic.

IV. The Thirty Years' War, 1618-1648

A. Introduction

European warfare between 1555 and 1648 combined the worst aspects of dynastic and religious conflict. Long years of dynastic struggle for hegemony and internal religious strife came to a head in the Thirty Years' War.

B. Bohemia Revolts

The Holy Roman Empire remained fragmented religiously and politically. The Peace of Augsburg guaranteed to each prince the right to determine the religious orthodoxy of his principality. The empire remained, as it had since the Golden Bull of 1356, decentralized. At the beginning of the seventeenth century, the head of the empire, the Habsburg emperor, presided over the eastern states of Austria, Bohemia, and Hungary. To secure the succession for his Catholic nephew, Emperor Mathias granted the monarchy of Bohemia to Ferdinand Habsburg. A staunch Catholic, Ferdinand rapidly alienated the Protestant majority of his new kingdom. A group of Protestant nobles rebelled against Ferdinand's government and physically threw two officials out of a window in the royal palace. This assault, the Defenestration of Prague, signaled the start of Protestant revolts throughout the Habsburg domains. Spain immediately joined their imperial Habsburg relatives to put down the Bohemian rebellion. In 1619 Ferdinand succeeded Mathias as Holy Roman Emperor. At the same moment, Frederick of the Palatinate, a Protestant prince, accepted the vacant Bohemian throne. War between Ferdinand and Frederick was inevitable. The first stage of the conflict that became known as the Thirty Years' War was a complete victory for the Catholic allies over the Bohemian pretender. Ferdinand's forces conquered their adversaries at the Battle of White Mountain and sacked Bohemia, which was added once again to the Habsburg estates. The victory of the Catholic emperor caused Protestant princes to seek potential allies in case the ruler wished to press his advantage in the empire.

C. The War Widens

To meet the Spanish and imperial Habsburg challenge, a group of Protestant allies— England, Holland, Denmark, and some German principalities—determined to carry on the conflict. In 1626 a Danish army invaded the empire. Under the command of Albrecht von Wallenstein, the imperial forces easily dispatched the Danish threat. By 1629, the Danes withdrew as leaders of the Protestant coalition. The emperor used his military superiority to reduce the influence of Protestantism within the borders of the Holy Roman Empire. Toleration for Calvinists was revoked, and all lands taken from the Catholic Church had to be returned. German Protestants had little choice but to unite in opposition to the emperor. In 1630 Gustavus Adolphus of Sweden assumed the leadership of the scattered Protestant alliance. Sweden's monarch hoped both to defend the northern tier of German Protestant principalities and simultaneously to protect Swedish interests in the Baltic. A wartime atrocity at the Protestant city of Magdeburg galvanized the Protestant opposition. Saxony and Brandenburg, previously hesitant to join the conflict, entered on the side of the Swedes. By 1631 the Protestant forces were able to seize the initiative and invade Catholic territories. The Palatinate was recaptured and Catholic Bavaria fell to the Protestant invaders. In the midst of his success, Gustavus Adolphus was killed at the battle of Lutzen.

D. The Long Quest for Peace

The theater of war changed from central Europe to the west. In 1621 the Spanish renewed their war with the provinces of Holland. Distracted by the early stages of the Thirty Years' War, the Spanish were unable to bring all of their military forces to bear on Holland. The naval superiority of the Dutch led to a series of Spanish setbacks. The Dutch razed Spanish colonies and attacked the New World treasure fleets. In 1627 the expenses of warfare so strained the Spanish treasury that Philip III declared bankruptcy. France declared war on Spain in 1635. The primary location of war between France and Spain was the Spanish Netherlands. Neither side was able to gain a military advantage, but the effects of many years of war were harsher for the Spanish. The Dutch won another victory at sea over the Spanish fleet in 1639. At the same time, the Portuguese rebelled in order to regain their independence. By 1640 all of the rulers and major figures at the outset of the Thirty Years' War had died. Those who succeeded them wanted nothing more than to end the war. Unfortunately, each monarch wanted to gain an advantage out of the peace. Only in 1648 was the Peace of Westphalia hammered out. It generally recognized Protestant and French gains at the expense of the Habsburgs. Spain agreed irrevocably to Dutch statehood. Sweden gained its superiority over the Baltic ports of northern Germany. France gained territories in the Lower Palatinate that closed the Spanish military highway to the Low Countries. Within the empire, the terms of the Peace of Augsburg were restored and explicitly extended to include Calvinists. The powers of the emperor were further weakened in favor of the princes.

TIMELINE

Insert the following events into the timeline. This should help you to compare important historical events chronologically.

Defenestration of Prague   Twelve Years' Truce
Peace of Westphalia   Saint Bartholomew's Day Massacre
Calvinists begin revolt of Netherlands Edict of Nantes

1566	
1572	
1598	
1609	
1618	
1648	

TERMS, PEOPLE, EVENTS

The following terms, people, and events are important to your understanding of the chapter. Define each one.

Catherine de Medicis   Guise family   Francis II
Henry Bourbon   Huguenots   *politiques*
Saint Bartholomew's Day   Edict of Nantes   Duc de Conde
Catholic League   Philip II of Spain   Spanish Armada
revolt of the Netherlands   Duke of Alba   William of Orange
"Spanish fury"   Poland-Lithuania   Sigismund III
Time of Troubles   Michael Romanov   Gustav I Vasa
Charles IX   Christian IV   Thirty Years' War
Gustavus Adolphus   Defenestration of Prague Christian IV of Denmark
Albrecht von Wallenstein   battle of Lutzen   Peace of Westphalia

MAP EXERCISE

The following exercise is intended to clarify the geophysical environment and the spatial relationships among the important objects and places mentioned in the chapter.

1. What country was most threatened by the Habsburg Empire of Philip II? How does that help to explain the nature of European history in the sixteenth and seventeenth centuries?

2. Does religion explain the alliance systems of the Thirty Years' War?

3. Locate the following places on the map.

    Locate the various states belonging to Philip II.
    Mark the Protestant states of Europe with a "P," Catholic states with a "C.,"
    Poland-Lithuania
    Sweden

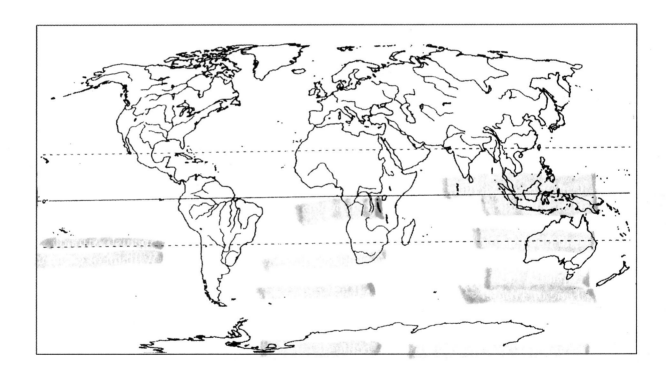

MAKING CONNECTIONS

The following questions are intended to emphasize important ideas within the chapter.

1. Why did the Reformation lead to internal violence in European states? What states were involved in internal religious wars?

2. What states engaged in the struggle for dominance around the Baltic? What state emerged as the most successful?

3. What were the causes of the Thirty Years' War? How did the emperor's success at the battle of the White Mountain lead to a wider conflict?

4. How did the final stages of the Thirty Years' War involve new nations in the conflict?

5. What was the solution to European violence in the Treaty of Westphalia?

PUTTING LARGER CONCEPTS TOGETHER

The following questions test your ability to summarize the major conclusions of the chapter.

1. In both France and the Spanish empire, religious wars involved a Catholic state against a Protestant rebellion. How were the two revolutions different? In what ways were they similar? Consider, for example, the results of each.

2. Was the Thirty Years' War dynastic or religious in nature? Explain the motives of each of the combatants for their involvement.

SELF-TEST OF FACTUAL INFORMATION

1. The power behind the throne during the French wars of religion was

    a. Lorenzo de' Medici.
    b. Philip II of Spain.
    c. Mary, Queen of Scots.
    d. Catherine de Medicis.

2. What family dominated the French offices of state under Francis II?

    a. the Medicis
    b. the Guises
    c. the Bourbons
    d. the Habsburgs

3. In the Saint Bartholomew's Day Massacre

    a. Henry Bourbon was assassinated.
    b. the Guises were assassinated.
    c. there was indiscriminate slaughter of Protestants, but most of the Huguenot leaders escaped.
    d. there was indiscriminate slaughter of Catholics, but most of the Catholic leaders escaped.

4. The *politiques* were Catholics who

    a. formed the Catholic League.
    b. desired a practical settlement of the civil wars.
    c. plotted the assassination of Henry Bourbon.
    d. joined the royal government in opposition to the Huguenots.

5. Henry Bourbon justified his conversion to Catholicism after succeeding to the French throne by saying,

    a. "I've been a Lutheran and a Calvinist. Why not a Catholic?"
    b. "God will forgive me."
    c. "Paris is worth a mass."
    d. "The kingdom of France is greater than any religion."

6. In 1609 Spain and the Netherlands concluded the

    a. Peace of Augsburg.
    b. Peace of Westphalia.
    c. Twelve Years' Truce.
    d. Defenestration of Prague.

7. Which of the following was initially a French Huguenot?

    a. Henry Guise
    b. Henry Bourbon of Navarre
    c. Catherine de Medicis
    d. Henry II

8. The Pacification of Ghent of 1576 included all of the following terms except

    a. local autonomy in taxation.
    b. the immediate withdrawal of all Spanish troops.
    c. the central role of the States-General in legislation.
    d. the independence of the northern states of Holland and Zeeland.

9. The selection of a monarch for what German kingdom precipitated the Thirty Years' War?

    a. Bavaria
    b. Bohemia
    c. the Palatinate
    d. Hanover

10. Which of the following was NOT a term included in the Treaty of Westphalia?

    a. Sweden gained further territories in the Baltic.
    b. Spain recognized the independence of Holland.
    c. The Peace of Augsburg was abandoned as the definition of religion within the Holy Roman Empire.
    d. The powers of the Holy Roman Emperor were weakened with respect to other German states.

CHAPTER 15

The Experiences of Life in Early Modern Europe, 1500-1650

OUTLINE

I.   Haymaking

Sixteenth-century life remained largely rural and agricultural. Men and women toiled in fields along with their neighbors. Housing was still constructed of wood and thatch. It was more spacious and comfortable than medieval domestic housing, but not by much. The parish church, the grandest building in an agricultural village, still dominated the rural landscape.

II.   Economic Life

A. Introduction

Sixteenth-century society varied from one region to another and from one social class to another. There was no typical European. The long-delayed population recovery from the Black Death transformed European society.

B. Rural Life

Villages varied in size from one hundred families in western Europe to twenty families in eastern Europe. Peasants made up the majority of the European population and were recruited by the state and aristocracy for labor and military service. Much of the income from the village went to the payment of taxes, rents, and tithes. Agricultural productivity was precarious. Crops barely sufficed to supply the agricultural village. Winter, crop diseases, and changes in weather were likely to result in food shortages. Peasant housing was crude, often consisting of a single long hall with a fireplace for heat and a single window to the outside world. Housing was shared during bad weather with animals. Peasant personal property was limited—a chest, a table, a bedstead, some pots and utensils. Peasant life was controlled by the agricultural seasons. In northern Europe, the primary organization of land was the three-field rotation in which winter wheat, spring crops, and fallow were alternated. Wheat was the commercial crop, while the peasants consumed bread made of the less valuable rye and barley. In the Mediterranean climatic region, a two-field rotation remained the rule. Grain crops were supplemented by Mediterranean luxury products—olives and grapes. In mountainous areas throughout Europe, animal husbandry was practiced. Sheep were the most common domesticated animal. In wooded areas, pigs were kept. The most common draught animal was the ox, bred in great numbers in eastern Europe. Most land was owned by the state, the Church, or the aristocracy. In western Europe, peasant land ownership was more common than in eastern Europe. In contrast, labor service as a condition of land tenure was much more common in the east than in the west. In general, western European peasants had greater social and economic mobility than their eastern counterparts. Within any village, there were variations in wealth and social status among the peasantry.

C. Town Life

If nature defined agricultural life, city life was an environment of human invention. Guilds continued to regulate the conditions of labor, as they did in the Middle Ages. Towns were more market-oriented than rural villages. Labor was exchanged for a greater variety of goods than in the countryside, although abject poverty remained a problem. Urban occupations were varied. In smaller towns the market in food items dominated exchange. Women often were prevalent in these trades. Smaller towns tended to be semi-agricultural with fields farmed by urban citizens. In larger towns, there was a greater variety of occupations. Wholesale merchants controlled the major crafts and markets, while individual households supplied unskilled labor. Crafts in larger towns were concentrated in specific quarters rather than spread randomly throughout the urban space. Even in larger towns, some tasks—midwifery, prostitution, and wet-nursing—were reserved for women. Most citizens survived by periodic employment as unskilled laborers. Domestic service was a common occupation. Towns survived on the basis of a regular supply of foodstuffs. To insure it, some towns owned agricultural lands. Grain was often stored in municipal warehouses, and urban councils strictly controlled food prices.

D. Economic Change

The catalyst for economic change was population growth throughout Europe. Cities tended to increase in population more rapidly than rural regions. Initially the population increase spurred economic growth. With more available labor, lands abandoned during the Black Death were brought back into cultivation. Agricultural productivity increased. Greater supplies of foodstuffs supported larger urban populations, which in turn increased the supply of manufactured goods. Increased population pressure eventually forced extension of the agricultural system to lands less fertile and to areas formerly reserved for animal husbandry. In some cases, actual colonization of the wilderness took place to meet the insatiable demand for foodstuffs. By the middle of the sixteenth century, the economic situation deteriorated. Crafts in the towns reached their labor saturation point. Guilds began to limit new admissions, and wages generally fell as the supply of workers increased. The decline in wages was more traumatic because of contemporary inflation. The so-called Price Revolution was the result of two events: the importation of vast quantities of bullion discovered in the New World and the widespread practice of debasing coinage. The impact of the Price Revolution was enormous. Grain prices climbed faster than those for manufactured goods, putting tremendous pressure on urban councils to hold the line on food prices. Those who held long-term contracts for rents suffered, while those who received payment in kind profited. Peasants who depended on the value of their labor for supplemental income were made destitute. In peasant communities, the social distinctions between those who owned land and those who did not became more pronounced. In eastern Europe, where peasant land ownership was uncommon, the aristocracy used the situation to further bind the peasantry in servitude. In the west, landless vagrants with little hope of employment wandered from village to village.

III. Social Life

A. Introduction

Sixteenth-century social life was stratified. People identified themselves with a particular group, rather than as individuals. The rapid economic change of the sixteenth century challenged the traditional social organization of Europe.

B. Social Constructs

Sixteenth-century society consisted of an interlocking set of hierarchies—within the nobility, crafts, urban government, even the household. Status largely determined one's position in the hierarchy. Social conventions dictating courtesy between various groups, manners of dress, and titles all were symbols of status. All things and people had a specific place in the hierarchy, a concept represented by the Great Chain of Being and reinforced in the political metaphor of the Body Politic. Status, according to the social theories of the day, was static.

C. Social Structure

European society was supposedly divided into two status groups—nobles and commoners. Nobility implied certain privileges, notably the title granted and the right to bear a coat of arms. The nobility also possessed political rights. Members of the nobility were, by their status, eligible for high office in the state and customarily summoned to representative institutions. Nobles also held economic advantages over commoners. In most cases, the nobility paid no taxes, a significant exclusion. In return for their favored status, nobles were expected to serve as military commanders. By the sixteenth century, the professionalization of warfare limited the military role of the nobility, but accentuated their administrative function. Between the nobility and the commoners, a new group without clear status was emerging. In function, it differed little from the nobility, although it did not enjoy either title or privilege. Urban elites tended to be members of this group. Some of the wealthiest and most powerful townsmen successfully transferred themselves to the lower levels of the nobility. In the countryside, those who were able to obtain greater quantities of land in the course of the sixteenth century clearly separated themselves from the class of agricultural laborers from which they sprang. This group is often referred to as the gentry. Even among the commoners, there were clear hierarchies of status usually related in rural villages to ownership of land or freedom from labor service. In towns status was connected to citizenship.

D. Social Change

The expansion of the state and the creation of new wealth unrelated to noble status placed stress on the European social system. In the long run, the hierarchies of social status were inevitably changed. On the positive side, noble titles increased as the population growth required more people eligible to govern. Employment in the state offered opportunities for wealth and advancement. For some, the Price Revolution proved to be a windfall. On the negative side, the population explosion dramatically increased the numbers of destitute. The burden of care of the poor fell on local communities. When the ability of local charities to care for the poor was exhausted, the state intervened. In many cases, the state was more concerned with the problem of controlling vagrancy than in alleviating the plight of the poor. Imprisonment and corporal punishments were imposed on vagrants.

E. Peasant Revolts

Changes in social organization led to conflict between the orders. Peasant revolts, although often moderate in purpose and well organized, were brutally suppressed. Many peasant revolts were in response to changes in the agricultural system imposed by surges and recessions in the economy. Protection of woodlands and enclosure of open fields for commercial agriculture provoked strong peasant responses. Both had deleterious effects on the small landholder. Peasant revolts broke out in Hungary in 1514, England in 1549, and Germany in 1525. The German revolt, although disowned by Martin Luther, combined an assault on both the secular and ecclesiastical nobility. Peasants objected to changes taking place in agricultural villages and demanded freedom from serfdom. Their desire for stability contradicted the volatile economy of the sixteenth century.

IV.   Private and Community Life

A. Introduction

Despite the revolutionary nature of sixteenth-century political and economic developments, there was continuity in private life. Strongest ties remained to family and local community.

B. The Family

Family was at the foundation of private life. In western Europe, the nuclear family was most common. In eastern Europe, the nuclear family was also prevalent, although extended households were more common than in the west. Kinship ties bound the family to other groups within rural communities. The family also stressed the relationship between past generations and the present. Among the nobility this tendency was more pronounced in the forms of inheritance and coats of arms, but it also existed in the transfer of land from one peasant generation to the next. The individual household was also an economic unit, with all members contributing their labor to its welfare. Households were subject to the authority of the adult parents. The husband was titular head, but children and servants were responsible to both husband and wife. Despite population growth, the size of the typical family remained small. Infant mortality and relatively late age of marriage for women depressed the birth rate. Women endured many pregnancies during their lives. The economic role of women within the household was varied. Wives prepared food, kept domestic animals, educated children and provided primary child care, made clothing, and cleaned. In towns women might add the tasks of selling goods and directing domestics. Men performed more public duties—the primary agricultural tasks, the construction of farm equipment, performance of owed labor services, and participation in the political life of the village. Marriage was the normal social condition for both men and women.

C. Communities

Households existed within a community structure, either rural or urban. Communities were organized by the secular and ecclesiastical lords. Rural lords established conditions of labor and land usage. The village church was both a spiritual and social center, a focal point for holidays and celebrations. Communities expressed their social solidarity by ceremonial activities in which all members of the village participated. In rural villages, priests led residents in annual perambulations of the lands. In towns, ceremonial processions were more formal and reflected the greater social stratification of urban life. Weddings were significant ceremonies for the entire community. Marriages bound families—and often wealth—together. They marked the admission of a new household to the community. Because property and community approval were involved, weddings were public affairs. Other festivals were associated with the passage of stages of the agricultural cycle. Festivals released community members from labor and presented opportunities to resolve community squabbles. Festivals also offered the chance for the social hierarchy of the community to be placed on public display.

D. Popular Beliefs and the Persecution of Witchcraft

Despite the print revolution, most Europeans remained illiterate. The common man's sense of the world around him was individual and experiential, not scientific. Not surprisingly, sixteenth-century society was imbued with the magical. Magical solutions abounded for medical problems, changes in the weather, disastrous harvests, and for prediction of future events. Use of magical powers for evil was considered witchcraft. Consultation with the black powers of evil spirits and the devil, himself, brought the repressive powers of the churches into play. Prosecutions for witchcraft became common in the sixteenth century. Women were most often the objects of prosecutions for witchcraft.

TERMS, PEOPLE, EVENTS

The following terms, people, and events are important to your understanding of the chapter. Define each one.

manorial rents	parish tithes	seigneur
black bread	*robot*	guilds
specialization of labor	domestic service	Price Revolution
Gdansk	hierarchy	status
Great Chain of Being	Body Politic	*Book of Gold*
Esch	villein	"deserving poor"
sturdy beggars	enclosure	Ket's Rebellion
Peasants' War	public sphere	domestic sphere
annual perambulation	processions	Carnival
rites of May	skimmingtons	witchcraft

MAKING CONNECTIONS

The following questions are intended to emphasize important ideas within the chapter.

1. What was the peasant household like? What was the nature of peasant agriculture? What was the relationship of the peasantry to the soil? How did this relationship differ between east and west?

2. How did town life differ from that of the agricultural village? How was the town linked to the village?

3. What were the two basic changes in the economy of sixteenth-century Europe? What were the causes of the Price Revolution? What was its effect on village and town?

4. What was the structure of sixteenth-century European society? On what metaphors was it based?

5. How did the family and the community serve to maintain social stability?

PUTTING LARGER CONCEPTS TOGETHER

The following questions test your ability to summarize the major conclusions of the chapter.

1. What were the elements of sixteenth-century life that mandated stability? How did these constructs and institutions limit change?

2. What were the elements of change in sixteenth-century Europe? Was change or stability more critical to sixteenth-century life?

SELF-TEST OF FACTUAL INFORMATION

1. Which of the following would NOT be typical in an average rural village?

    a. Farming was still a communal activity.
    b. The Protestant Reformation reduced the significance of the village church.
    c. Both men and women labored in the fields.
    d. Villages showed signs of population growth.

2. What distinguished Mediterranean agriculture from that of northern Europe?

    a. a two-field rotation
    b. no domesticated animals
    c. absence of cereal crops
    d. absence of the vine and the grape

3. Labor service was

    a. dying out as a relationship between lord and peasant all over Europe.
    b. more common in than in the east.
    c. enforced by the European states to control vagrancy.
    d. more common in eastern Europe than in the west.

4. Which of the following was NOT a change in the agricultural system brought about by the population increase?

    a. Poorer lands were abandoned as more intensive effort was placed on fertile areas.
    b. Animal flocks diminished as less land was available for animal husbandry.
    c. Colonization of previously uninhabited areas took place.
    d. Woodlands were diminished.

5. Which of the following did NOT occur during the Price Revolution?

    a. Grain prices rose faster than those of manufactured goods.
    b. Landlords with long-term rents suffered
    c. Landlords who received payment in kind benefited
    d. Wages continued to rise throughout the century.

6. Which of the following was NOT a challenge to traditional social organization in the sixteenth century?

    a. the rise to wealth and prominence of new social groups
    b. rising numbers of rural and urban poor
    c. migration of large numbers of people to New World colonies
    d. transformation of landholding patterns in villages 160

7. Which of the following was NOT a factor causing changes at the top of the social scale?

    a. new wealth created by the Price Revolution
    b. opportunities for advancement in state service
    c. the need for more governors due to the population increase
    d. the tendency to pass titles on to all male children

8. Magical practices

    a. were restricted to the poor and illiterate.
    b. were limited to circles of witches and sorcerers.
    c. appealed to people at all levels of society.
    d. were virtually unknown in the sixteenth century.

9. The most common targets of investigation for magical practices were

    a. the insane.
    b. children.
    c. men.
    d. women.

10. Which of the following community activities was a celebration of the community's dead?

    a. perambulation
    b. All Hallows' Eve
    c. Carnival
    d. rites of May

CHAPTER 16

The Royal State in the Seventeenth Century

OUTLINE

I.   Fit for a King

Versailles represented the power, prestige, and wealth of the state. Built at extraordinary expense, Versailles became the architectural persona of Louis XIV's absolutism. So intent was the monarch on creating a public image that the private accommodations were meager and uncomfortable. In the same fashion, the majesty of Louis XIV's France was a veneer over the poverty and unhappiness of some of his people.

II.   The Rise of the Royal State

A. Introduction

Warfare at the outset of the seventeenth century was, itself, a cause for the development of a more centralized state.

B. Divine Kings

In the seventeenth century, monarchs became the personification of the power of the state. Palaces and capital cities magnified the public aura of kings. Portraiture was utilized to express royal majesty. Literature and history were subordinated to the glorification of monarchy. Royalty was elevated to the level of mythos. Political theory matched the arts. The divine right of kings held that God created the institution of monarchy and appointed kings as his representatives on earth to ensure good order. King James I actually wrote a treatise on the divine right of monarchs entitled *The True Law of Free Monarchies*. More surprisingly, the theory of rule through heavenly appointment was generally accepted outside the circle of monarchs. In order to properly exercise the powers ordained by God, a monarch had to act in the best interests of his people—rule through good laws, pursue peace and prosperity. Kings who failed to rule according to divine dictates—whatever they were perceived to be—risked God's wrath. Kings became synonymous with the public performance of the duties of state, and all monarchs were constrained to appear in front of their subjects.

C. The Court and the Courtiers

In fact, the duties of government in the seventeenth century were larger in scope than one man or woman could possibly handle. Consequently, more state officers were required to manage the growing burden of government. As courts expanded, once independent aristocrats were co-opted into royal service. Royal councillors grew in wealth, prestige, and power as they gained the ability to create executive policy. The point of contact between monarch and royal council was often a personal favorite—either an officially appointed chief minister or simply a personal companion with more frequent access to the king or queen. Favorites were often shields for monarchs against public displeasure with royal policies. A number of men best represent the powers and dangers of becoming a royal Favorite. In France the most powerful official of the royal government during the reign of Louis XIII was Cardinal Richelieu. During his early political career, Richelieu enjoyed the patronage of Marie de Medicis, mother of Louis XIII. As chief minister of France, the cardinal took over the most burdensome governmental duties of the monarch leaving Louis free to pursue less arduous pastimes. A brilliant manager of public affairs, Richelieu undertook the tasks of state centralization. His success earned him many powerful enemies, but he died in office in 1642. Count-Duke Olivares succeeded to his family's titles and fortunes. Rather unusually, Olivares also obtained a university education. Olivares' power was attributable to his position as personal favorite of Philip IV of Spain with immediate access to the monarch. Olivares, like his French rival Richelieu, was intent on the construction of a centralized monarchy. Unfortunately for him, the failure of his aggressive foreign policy led to his dismissal from office in 1643. James I elevated the Duke of Buckingham from the ranks of the commoners to the nobility of England. Buckingham's position as the royal favorite allowed him to gain influence within the royal government, particularly in the military. Buckingham survived the death of James I to become the royal favorite of Charles I. His continued role of influence and power within the royal court alienated many of the English nobility. When his foreign policy schemes failed, Parliament attempted to have him removed from the king's presence. The support of the monarch frustrated parliamentary attempts at impeachment, but a disgruntled naval officer assassinated Buckingham in 1628.

D. The Drive to Centralize Government

Despite the attempts of monarchs and personal favorites to increase the power of the central government, powerful regional elements existed within all the states of western Europe. One of the primary means of achieving centralization over the regions was the creation of strong central legal systems. In France, the *parlement* (or high court of appeals) expanded in the seventeenth century. Royal justice was extended to the various districts of France, as the number of regional *parlements* increased. As courts grew, so did the influence of professional lawyers. Similarly in Spain, those with legal training, known as *letrados*, entered the administration of the kingdom. In England the growth of regional courts outdistanced the development of the central court system. The monarchy delegated the responsibility for local court systems to members of the local elite who were named justices of the peace. Justices were required to maintain law and order in the countryside until the arrival of one of the judges of the central courts. In addition to the extension of legal systems, it was necessary for monarchs to appoint new officials to represent royal interests in the provinces. In France, the *intendants* began to replace the aristocratic provincial governors, who spent much of their time in Paris rather than in the countryside. *Intendants* were not normally part of the regional aristocracy in the districts they governed. As a result, they were more responsive to the needs of the central administration. The local officials in England were called Lords Lieutenant. England, alone among European states, was without a standing national army. The function of the Lords Lieutenant was to raise, equip, and train a local militia on royal demand. Needless to say, English armies were not the most proficient in Europe. In Spain regionalism was more problematic than France or England. Catalonia, in particular, insisted on the maintenance of its additional separatism and regional rights. Olivares was unable to overcome the centrifugal tendencies of the Spanish regions. Catalonia eventually rebelled against the central government.

E. The Taxing Demands of War

War and the taxation it required was the engine that drove state consolidation. Taxation also produced opposition to the royal administration from all levels of European society. Armies increased in size, artillery and gunpowder were new and necessary expenses, and food and fodder rose in cost. Military action caused real economic hardship in terms of damages for those in the path of marauding armies, increases in food prices, and raised taxes. Exclusion of the nobility from taxation in the western states caused the burden of taxation to fall on those least able to afford it. States resorted to all sorts of stratagems to increase their income. England's constitution required the monarch to receive the approval of Parliament before initiating new taxes. Despite governmental shortfalls, Parliament proved hesitant to approve taxation. Most royal revenue was derived from customs duties on luxury imports. In the 1630s, Charles I attempted to impose an ancient duty that required ports to supply ships in times of naval crisis on all English towns, even those far from the water. The gentry generally refused to accept the royal innovation and took the royal government to court in a constitutional challenge of the king's right to tax.

III. The Crises of the Royal State

A. Introduction

The expansion of the state occurred at the expense of other corporate entities—the Church, towns, and aristocracy. Often immune from taxation, the corporate bodies nevertheless relied on their own ability to mulct the peasantry. More efficient and intrusive legal systems disrupted the traditional patterns of local authority. At the same time, population pressure on the agricultural system led to failures in the food supply. Responses were violent. At first resistance was on a local level. By the 1640s, the focus of resistance was the state itself and the concept of divine monarchy.

B. The Need to Resist

Disease, crop failure, and the effects of war on noncombatants caused European population to decline in the seventeenth century. In the early seventeenth century all segments of the economy stagnated. Poor weather contributed to setbacks in agriculture that were most devastating to the peasantry and led to disorder and rebellion. Most revolts were directed against local tax collectors and strictly limited in objective. In England, local resistance was aimed at halting the progress of enclosure of open fields. In the kingdom of Naples, the shortage of food in the city of Palermo led to rebellion. When the disorder forced the government to abolish the tax on foods, similar revolts broke out in the city of Naples. Success for rebels was short-lived. The royal government suppressed both movements.

C. The Right to Resist

Peasant rebellions, generally opposed by local elites, could not succeed in the face of national armies. Only when the aristocracy joined in the cause of rebellion could the state be threatened. The right to rebel developed in curious combination with the theories of divine monarchy. As kings were God's representatives on earth, it became not only possible but necessary to dethrone tyrants—those who did not rule according to the divine strictures of upholding justice and piety. The duty of rebellion fell at first on lesser magistrates and members of the elite, but later was extended to all members of the Body Politic. Attempts to murder James I of England failed, but in 1610 Henry IV of France did fall to an assassin. John Milton completed the theory of righteous rebellion by adding the concept of a contract between monarch and the governed. In *The Tenure of Kings and Magistrates*, Milton suggested that if kings failed in their contractual obligations to rule well, citizens could dissolve the contractual relationship between themselves and the ruler to reconstitute the state. The theoretical justification of rebellion was put into practice in the Spanish dominions in 1640. In that year, both Portugal and Catalonia rejected the authority of the Spanish monarch. Portugal, only recently added to Spanish possessions, achieved its goal of independence. Catalonia, long a part of unified Spain, represented a more serious threat to Olivares' attempts at state consolidation. The Catalan elite embraced what was initially a peasants' rebellion and declared the contractual relationship between themselves and Philip IV dissolved. Despite French intervention, the Catalan revolt failed. Like Spain, the French government was virtually bankrupt by 1640. When Louis XIV succeeded to the throne as a minor, the government under the direction of Anne of Austria and Cardinal Mazarin chose to raise taxes on officeholders and the aristocracy. When the *Parlement* of Paris refused to register the new taxes, the confrontation between royal government and the regional elite was inevitable. The Fronde, as the aristocratic rebellion was called, threatened an appeal to Spanish intervention in order to force concessions from Mazarin. Unwilling to agree on a program of constitutional reform and unable to control the deterioration of order in the cities of France, the Fronde lost its popular mandate. The royal government was swiftly restored.

D. The English Civil War

The most severe disruption of monarchical rule occurred in the least likely of countries, England. James I, the king of Scotland, succeeded Elizabeth without dissension in 1603. Initial resistance to the Crown arose over the elevation of Scottish favorites to English offices. In addition, the royal government was forced to operate without a sufficient tax base. Requests to Parliament for additional revenues produced parliamentary demands for reform. In 1628, Parliament issued the Petition of Right restating the traditional freedoms of the English elite. In response, Charles I chose not to call a Parliament between 1629 and 1640. Adding to the dissatisfaction with the royal government was unhappiness with the state church. Puritans demanded a more Calvinist form of religion, including the abolition of the episcopacy of the Anglican Church. James I and his successor Charles I both saw the bishops as part of the hierarchy of the state and refused to abolish them. Both monarchs attempted to strengthen the authority of the bishops, not to reduce it. In Archbishop William Laud, the Anglican Church received a conservative head bent on a more formal liturgy in contradiction to the Puritans' demands for a more rigorous brand of Calvinism. When a new prayer book to which all churches were supposed to conform was introduced in Scotland in 1637, the Scottish nobility refused to allow its imposition. When Charles I tried to gain parliamentary taxes to support military suppression of the religious and political uprising in Scotland, it refused. The Long Parliament first met in 1640. Instead of granting fiscal support, the Parliament demanded constitutional reform and the removal of specific royal councillors. Archbishop Laud was imprisoned. Charles' chief political advisor, the earl of Strafford, was executed. When Charles' belated and clumsy attempt to arrest leading members of the Long Parliament failed, the king withdrew from his capital in 1642 to raise a royal army. Parliament also called for military support to confront the king's military. The king was able to gain the support of much of the English aristocracy. Parliament enjoyed the support of those who sought religious reform. By 1645 parliamentary forces gained a military advantage. Charles I, actually a prisoner of Parliament, refused to cooperate with his conquerors. In the face of royal intransigence, the uneasy coalition of opponents of the Crown began to disintegrate. Religious moderates and radicals created new political alignments.

E. The English Revolution

Religious radicals were concentrated in the parliamentary army, which in 1647 became the central force in prosecuting the rebellion against royal authority. The army and its commanders easily defeated remaining royalist forces. When it appeared that moderates in Parliament might seek a new agreement with Charles I, the army invaded London and purged moderates from the representative body. The remaining radicals in Parliament, called the Rump, brought the king to trial and convicted him of tyranny. Charles' execution in 1649 led to the abolition of monarchy and the establishment of a cornmonwealth under the remainder of the lower house of Parliament. The Rump was unable to create a viable constitution. When the Rump's failure became obvious, Oliver Cromwell, commander of the army, expelled the remnants of the Long Parliament. Cromwell adopted the title of Lord Protector under a new constitution called the Instrument of Government of 1653. Cromwell refused the offer of a crown and attempted to govern through Parliament and the Council of State. After Cromwell's death, there was no viable candidate to succeed him as Protector. In 1659 army commanders called for the restoration of the monarchy. After lengthy negotiations, Charles II, son of Charles I, returned to England in 1660. The restored monarchy was forced to recognize the authority of Parliament and the limitations of royal power. Both the state religion and the limited authority of the crown were challenged in the reign of James II. When the king attempted to openly support Catholicism, virtually all elements of English authority rejected the monarchy. In 1688, with the encouragement of many in England, William of Orange and his wife, Mary Stuart, invaded. With virtually no support, James II had little choice but go into exile. Parliament recognized William and Mary as joint monarchs to govern under an agreement called the Declaration of Rights. The so-called Glorious Revolution of 1688 produced a new political theorist, John Locke. In *Two Treatises on*

Civil Government, Locke proposed a social contract that existed between rulers and their subjects. In the contract, the governed gave up some of their unlimited natural rights to the ruler in order to secure greater liberty and freedom from violence. Monarchs who acted arbitrarily or failed to protect the rights of their subjects could be deposed.

IV. The Zenith of the Royal State

A. Introduction

In the aftermath of the mid-century rebellions, the search for political stability became a primary goal of monarchs and regional political elites. Royal reforms of administrative policy were balanced by a greater willingness on the part of the regional elites to cooperate with the central government. While England, Holland, and Sweden developed balanced constitutions that limited the role of the monarchy, elsewhere the rule of government was royal absolutism.

B. The Nature of Absolute Monarchy

Most countries were unwilling to grant the degree of political freedom necessary for the operation of a balanced constitution. More common was the development of absolute monarchy along the lines developed by Thomas Hobbes. In *Leviathan*, Hobbes theorized that humans in a "state of nature" engaged in constant warfare. To avoid such internecine strife, men gave up their rights to rulers who undertook the restoration of law and order, the only guarantee of individual rights. Absolutism involved reverence for the person of the monarch as the symbol of the state, the consequent diminution of other elites within the state, personal management of the government by the ruler, decline of influence of representative bodies, and growth of the military. Absolutism remained more theoretical than practical. It depended on a capable ruler, the absence of religious divisions, and the will of the governed to support the government.

C. Absolutism in the East

One of the most successful absolute monarchies existed in the newly created state of Brandenburg-Prussia. Frederick William took over the region in the tragic aftermath of the Thirty Years' War. Without a tax base, with a population devastated by the religious wars, and with the aristocracy (the *Junkers*) virtually independent, Frederick William had little foundation for absolutism. He first instituted an excise tax, then built a strong national army controlled through a national war department. Russia, too, established absolutism in the wake of military reform. Tsar Peter I determined to adopt western European patterns of political organization and modeled his national army after that of Brandenburg-Prussia. After numerous failures, the military reforms resulted in the defeat of Sweden at the battle of Poltava in 1709. Peter also compelled the emulation of western European patterns of dress and appearance. In public administration, Peter divided Russia into regional districts controlled by royally-appointed officers. He also subjugated the church to the power of the state and confiscated much of its wealth.

D. The Origins of French Absolutism

Cardinal Richelieu was the architect of absolutism in France. Richelieu attempted to neutralize what he perceived as the three greatest threats to the French state: the position of the Huguenots in positions of power, the independence of the aristocracy, and the freedom of action enjoyed by regional governors. Richelieu brought the nobility under the rule of law, appointed *intendants* to undercut the authority of regional governors, and revoked the privileges of self-government jealously guarded by the Huguenots. Richelieu's policies of centralization brought on the Fronde.

E. Louis le Grand

Richelieu's foundation for absolutism was advanced during the reign of Louis XIV. During the king's minority, Cardinal Mazarin tutored the young monarch in statecraft. The cleric brought the Fronde to a close and continued the war against Spain. In 1661, Louis personally assumed the tasks of government without a chief minister. He was served, however, by powerful assistants. Jean-Baptiste Colbert directed the financial aspects of France and led the country to solvency through greater efficiency. The Marquis de Louvois was responsible for the development of the military. He enacted reforms in logistical organization, the command structure, and recruitment. Louis intentionally excluded the old nobility of the sword from public administration. Ministers managed departments of state through small councils of professional bureaucrats. The connection between the central government and the provinces remained the *intendant*, an office that became even more important under Louis XIV. Louis played the part of state symbol better than any other monarch. Versailles became the facade for statecraft. The French aristocracy was emasculated through required service at the royal palace where they were reduced to enacting complex rituals of etiquette. The appearance of Versailles established Louis' court as the most majestic in Europe. French culture was widely emulated elsewhere in the capitals of kings. Absolutism depended on the capability of the king: Louis, though able to create a magnificent stage on which absolutism was played, bankrupted France through an aggressive foreign policy. The king also renewed the persecution of Protestants, creating an embittered minority committed to the destruction of French absolutism.

TIMELINE

Insert the following events into the timeline. This should help you to compare important historical events chronologically.

end of the Fronde	Russians win battle of Poltava
execution of Charles I	Glorious Revolution in England
revolution in Palermo	Catalan rebellion

1640	
1647	
1649	
1652	
1688	
1709	

TERMS, PEOPLE, EVENTS

The following terms, people, and events are important to your understanding of the chapter. Define each one.

Ben Jonson	William Shakespeare	James I of England
True Law of Free Monarchies	Jean Bodin	favorite
Cardinal Richelieu	Count-Duke Olivares	Duke of Buckingham
letrados	justice of the peace	assizes
intendants	Lords Lieutenant	Ship Money
Nu-pieds	Philippe Duplessis-Mornay	John Milton
Catalan rebellion	The Fronde	Cardinal Mazarin
Petition of Right	Puritans	William Laud
Long Parliament	Oliver Cromwell	Rump Parliament
Instrument of Government	Divine right of kings	Glorious Revolution
Declaration of Rights	Toleration Act	John Locke
contract theory	absolutism	Thomas Hobbes
Frederick William	*Junker*	Peter I the Great
battle of Poltava	*raison d'etat*	Jean-Baptiste Colbert
Parlement	Versailles	Louis XIV of France

MAP EXERCISE

The following exercise is intended to clarify the geophysical environment and the spatial relationships among the important objects and places mentioned in the chapter.

1. What geographic element characterizes those states with limited or constitutional monarchies? What impact would dependence on the sea have on the nature of government? [Consider, for example, the role of merchants.]

2. What form of government was more typical of the previously decentralized portions of central Europe? What explanation could account for this fact?

3. Locate the following places on the map.

    the states with limited or constitutional monarchies.
    the states with more absolute forms of government.

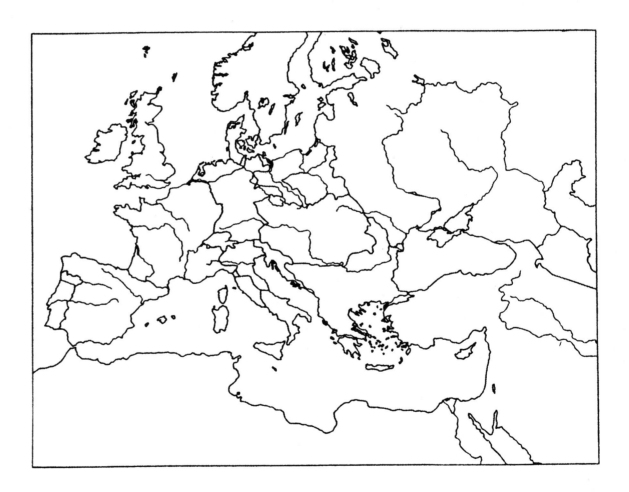

MAKING CONNECTIONS

The following questions are intended to emphasize important ideas within the chapter.

1. What was the "divine right of kings"? To what extent was it accepted in Europe?

2. How did divine right theory affect the structure of government? What was the role of favorites?

3. How did warfare affect monarchies?

4. What were the origins of the royal crises of the seventeenth century? What theories were elaborated that permitted resistance to the monarchy?

5. What factors account for the rebellions in England? What was their result? How did the Glorious Revolution lead to the development of Locke's social contract?

6. What was the nature of royal absolutism?

7. What was absolutism in eastern Europe initially based on?

8. What was the basis for French absolutism? How did Louis XIV complete the creation of absolute government? How successful was it?

PUTTING LARGER CONCEPTS TOGETHER

The following questions test your ability to summarize the major conclusions of the chapter.

1. In what ways did the concept of statehood change in Europe during the seventeenth century? What were the elements of the new state as it emerged under Louis XIV?

2. Was the concept of royal absolutism accepted everywhere in Europe? What theories were developed to support it? What theories attacked?

SELF-TEST OF FACTUAL INFORMATION

1. Which did NOT result from the increasing significance of war in the seventeenth century?

    a. the loss of royal authority
    b. the growth of the size of royal armies
    c. the increased importance of defense to governments' functions
    d. the erosion of the traditional privileges of the towns

2. All of the following were artists associated with royal portraiture except

    a. Diego Velazquez.
    b. Peter Paul Rubens.
    c. Ben Jonson.
    d. Anthony Van Dyck.

3. The local county courts of England were referred to as

    a. Chancery.
    b. Common Pleas.
    c. King's Bench.
    d. assizes.

4. Which of the following statements concerning royal taxation in the seventeenth century is most accurate?

    a. England was able to escape the cycle of increased military activity and raised taxes.
    b. Most taxes were equitably distributed among all ranks of European society.
    c. In Spain and France much of the wealth was beyond the reach of royal taxation.
    d. Most regimes were successful in reforming national systems of taxation.

5. Which of the following was NOT a cause of increased public dissatisfaction with royal government in the seventeenth century?

    a. increased taxation
    b. the absence of local officials
    c. bad harvests
    d. social and economic regulations

6. The aristocratic rebellion in France against the regency government of Cardinal Mazarin and Anne of Austria was called the

   a. Fronde.
   b. Catalan rebellion.
   c. Sicilian Vespers.
   d. Jacquerie.

7. Which of the following did NOT result from the English Civil War?

   a. Parliament became a permanent part of civil government and had to be managed rather than ignored.
   b. Religious toleration became the rule.
   c. Royal power over taxation was curtailed.
   d. Absolute monarchy became constitutional monarchy.

8. Who was responsible for the development of the contract theory of government as it developed in England after 1688?

   a. James II
   b. John Locke
   c. Thomas Hobbes
   d. Oliver Cromwell

9. Which of the following states did NOT develop royal absolutism?

   a. England
   b. Prussia
   c. France
   d. Russia

10. Which of the following was NOT considered by Richelieu to be a threat to the establishment of absolutism in France?

    a. the fact that Huguenots shared the state
    b. the independent power of the provincial officials
    c. the long tradition of aristocratic independence from royal authority
    d. the unwillingness of Louis XIV to engage in personal government

CHAPTER 17

Science and Commerce in Early Modern Europe

OUTLINE

I. Rembrandt's Lessons

    The commercial success of Holland created a dynamic society based on trade and governed by merchants. The wealth generated through the development of a commercial, seaborne empire allowed Holland, despite its diminutive size, to become one of Europe's cultural centers. Rembrandt van Rijn was the leading artist of seventeenth-century Holland. Rembrandt was famed for his use of group portraiture and innovative composition. In Holland political freedoms also led to more open investigation of previously forbidden scientific topics.

II. The New Science

    A. Introduction

       After two centuries of slavishly parroting the findings of classical scientists, the new science called the Aristotelian and Ptolemaic systems of antiquity into question. The new science of the seventeenth century depended on hypotheses different from those of the ancients—that the universe consisted of matter and that all relationships in the universe could be measured and recorded through the use of mathematics. The new science raged through educational institutions throughout Europe. It was not limited to one corner of the continent. Nor was the new science confined to the educational systems. The printing press carried the startling conclusions to the public.

    B. Heavenly Revolutions

       Aristotle had defined a timeless and perfect cosmology. It conformed well to the notions of the Great Chain of Being and the Body Politic. Unfortunately, Aristotle's system, even as expanded upon by Ptolemy, failed to coincide with astronomical observation of movement of the planets. The new science proposed radical departures from the Aristotelian cosmology. Nicolaus Copernicus of Poland suggested that placing the sun rather than the earth at the center of the planetary system better explained observable phenomena. In Denmark, Tycho Brahe made more exact observations of the heavens that demonstrated the insubstantiality of the paths along which the planets moved. One of Brahe's students, Johannes Kepler, used mathematics to describe the elliptical paths that marked the planets' voyages around the sun. With use of a telescope, the Italian astronomer Galileo made visual observations of the heavens previously impossible. More importantly, he publicized Copernicus' theory of a heliocentric universe. In 1633 the Catholic Church tried Galileo for heresy and forced him to recant his belief in a sun-centered cosmology.

C. The Natural World

The new science was determined to develop systems of thought that more accurately reflected observations in the natural world. During the Renaissance, Platonic idealism—the belief that ideas or forms best expressed reality—was resuscitated in Italy. Because numbers were themselves incorporeal (how can one show the number "two" in the natural world?), mathematics became the chief means of explaining natural phenomena. Numbers were the language of astronomers, alchemists, astrologers, and mystic numerologists who sought the secrets of the universe in combinations of numbers. Most influential of numerologists was Paracelsus, an alchemist who believed that all matter consisted of combinations of salt, sulfur, and mercury. While bizarre, Paracelsus' "science" challenged Aristotelian teachings on the composition of matter and medicine. Paracelsus' rejection of Aristotelian knowledge led others to more rational discoveries. Robert Boyle of England proposed the atomic structure of all matter and described accurately the relationship between volume and pressure of a gas. Medical knowledge was also advanced through a more precise study of anatomy. William Harvey, also of England, discovered the function of the heart as a pump to distribute blood throughout the body. Sir Isaac Newton of England best summarized the advances of the new science. Newton described the composition of light, developed the mathematical calculus, and constructed a reflecting telescope. Using earlier studies of Galileo, Newton expanded the physical theories of motion and inertia. Related to the laws of motion was the principle of attraction and repulsion that governed the movement of the planets—gravity.

D. Science Enthroned

The new science attracted royal patronage that financed the construction of centers of research. Royal societies were formed in England and France to bring together scientific minds. New schools, the mechanical colleges, arose to educate according to the dictates of the new science. In England, Sir Francis Bacon supported the scientific movement and advocated careful recording of scientific experimentation. Not everyone embraced the new science so enthusiastically. The Roman Catholic Church viewed the new trends in scientific discovery as simple heresy. Indeed, the rejection of the ancients led to widespread skepticism that anything could be known—either through revelation or science. Faith and reason seemed to be at odds. Rene Descartes attempted to bridge the gulf between the mystic and the knowable. Trained in the new science, Descartes was dismayed at the Church's condemnation of the teachings of Galileo—especially because Descartes' own mathematical discoveries agreed with those of the Italian. Descartes then produced a philosophical system, Cartesianism, devoted to explaining the relationship between the material and spiritual worlds. His explanation appeared in 1637 in *Discourse on Method*.

III. Empires of Goods

   A. Introduction

   The discovery of the New World and the establishment of colonial ventures there revolutionized the commercial world of the sixteenth and seventeenth centuries. The development of long-distance trade, whether to the New World, the Orient, or eastern Europe, caused changes in the technology of doing business and created new international trade rivalries.

   B. The Marketplace of the World

   The long-distance trade of the seventeenth century produced a unified intercontinental marketplace. Slaves from Africa mined South American silver, which was exported to Europe and used to purchase spices and other luxuries from Asia. There were no new trade routes opened or new technologies invented to account for the increase in trade. Instead, better organization and more efficient management of resources led to the commercial revolution. Triangular trade, in which goods passed from one market to a second in exchange for yet other commodities that were in demand in a third, expanded the range of trade items. Even more important were innovations in the creation of investment capital. The Bank of Amsterdam became the center of European finance through the development of giro, or transfer, banking. New financial notes, such as bills of exchange, made commercial transactions easier. The notes themselves became negotiable, thus a form of currency. The Bank of England, funded on taxes devoted to supporting the issue of bank notes, bought up other commercial paper in exchange for their own. Despite commercial advances, much of trade was still managed and capitalized within families. Trade offered the promise of high profits, but only at the risk of total loss.

   C. Consumption Choices

   Long-distance trade changed the shape of European consumption from luxury goods such as spices and silks to a broader range of exotic products. From the East, European bullion purchased spices exchanged in a triangular trade with Japan and the Indian subcontinent for silks, coffee, jewels, jade, porcelain, and other goods. The Dutch were the first to appreciate the potential of trade in Indian cotton cloth, called calicoes. By the middle of the eighteenth century, the English surpassed the Dutch in the calico trade. The Dutch and English both figured prominently in the coffee trade as well. Even more popular in Europe than coffee as a new beverage was tea. The English imported almost all tea from China in exchange for bullion. They later uncovered a market in China for opium that relieved the negative balance of trade. Tea drinking created a demand for sugar. In Brazil and the Caribbean, New World colonies raised sugar cane with African slave labor. The demand for sugar that could only be produced with slave labor created an enormous triangular trade system linking the New World, Africa, and Europe. Over six million black slaves were exported to the Americas in the eighteenth century. Over time, the British came to monopolize the trade in human labor. Along with sugar, the New World provided the markets of Europe with fish, furs, rice, and tobacco—the only native American plant product to find a market in Europe. The new products revolutionized the patterns of consumption in Europe.

D. Dutch Masters

The Dutch, alone among European countries, appeared to profit from the long years of war between 1565 and the Peace of Westphalia. Sea warfare proved less expensive than land campaigns. In addition, Holland attracted many skilled Protestants driven from neighboring Catholic countries. At the heart of Dutch prosperity was commerce. The Dutch Republic contained seventeen provinces, but the province of Holland was the most prosperous. The capital city of Amsterdam was a banking and commercial center that drew men and money to Holland. Dutch commercial success rested on naval superiority and the dominance Dutch shipping enjoyed in carrying goods of all nations. Dutch masters controlled the trade of the Baltic and of the East Indies throughout the seventeenth century. Only in the New World, where their colonial possessions were limited to the Hudson River, were the Dutch behind their European trade rivals. Dutch businessmen pioneered triangular trade and exchange banking. They were first to utilize marine insurance and joint stock markets to distribute the risks of investment. There were many factors that account for Dutch leadership in commercial innovation. The Dutch territories were small and produced insufficient supplies of food, thus necessitating trade. Dutch society was generally tolerant and attracted those who required a freer environment for inquiry and experimentation. Thus many of the intellectual elite found their way to the Dutch Republic, where they fostered an atmosphere of creativity.

E. Mercantile Organization

Outside the Dutch Republic, monarchs directed economic development for their own benefit. Trade was one of the least objectionable tax bases. Also, monarchs came to regard competition in trade as a means of weakening rivals without resorting to the expense of war. Trade competition resulted in the formulation of an economic doctrine called mercantilism. There were two fundamental assumptions in mercantilism: a nation's wealth was measured in its supplies of bullion, and what one nation gained from successful trade another nation inevitably lost. Mercantilism led to various stratagems to regulate trade. Bullion exportation was commonly forbidden. Monarchs granted monopolies over trading regions or items of trade in exchange for fees or as payoffs for political support. Two examples of trade monopolies were the English and Dutch East India companies. Both were joint-stock companies—that is, capital was raised for investment by selling shares of stock entitling investors to a share of the profits proportional to the amount of stock they owned. Both of the East India companies were financial successes, but most joint-stock operations failed to produce profits. Governments also passed laws to protect markets from foreign competition. In the 1660s the English passed the Navigation Acts which required colonial goods to be carried in English ships. The legislation was extremely successful, resulting in increased trade and a boom for English shipbuilding. The French also protected domestic markets by passage of legislation similar to the English Navigation Acts. In addition, French ministers raised tariffs on imported goods to stimulate French industries. The English shortly followed the French example. Both French and English protective legislation was aimed at the Dutch and their naval superiority.

IV.   The Wars of Commerce

   A. Introduction

   Protective legislation led to another round of international warfare. Mercantilism implied a form of economic warfare that pitted one state against another. Commercial superiority posed a national threat to less successful states.

   B. The Mercantile Wars

   The initial confrontation occurred between Holland and England, competitors for trade in the Orient and in the Atlantic. In the middle of the seventeenth century, while the British were engaged in their civil war, the Dutch expelled them from some of the most lucrative Asian markets. A series of three naval wars followed. The preponderance of Dutch ships were outfitted strictly for commerce. Despite the numerical superiority of their navy, the Dutch had fewer military ships than did the English. In the course of warfare, Dutch commercial superiority was lost. Their last New World colony, New Amsterdam, fell to the English. Only the Glorious Revolution and the succession in England of the Dutch Prince William of Orange brought the conflict to a close. The French struck at Dutch commercial superiority through a system of protective tariffs. Dependent on free trade, the Dutch suffered more than the French in the contest to erect tariff walls. Louis XIV's plans to gain the Spanish Netherlands were more militant than Colbert's economic warfare. Louis invaded the Netherlands until forced to withdraw by a coalition of European states.

   C. The Wars of Louis XIV

   Louis XIV pursued an aggressive foreign policy that brought him into conflict with virtually every other European state. Much of the warfare renewed the old antipathies between France and the territories of the Habsburgs—Spain, the Spanish Netherlands, and the Holy Roman Empire. Against the French designs, ambassadors of other nations constructed a balance of power—a coalition of forces that together matched the power of France. In 1688 French aggression on the borders of the Holy Roman Empire precipitated war, pitting France against the empire, England, and Holland. The Nine Years' War that followed failed to resolve the diplomatic problems of French expansion. The war, ended by the Peace of Ryswick in 1697, did provide evidence that concerted action on the part of the Grand Alliance could restrain French aggression if it could not end it. The second outbreak of warfare occurred as a result of dynastic failure in the kingdom of Spain. As it became widely recognized that Charles II of Spain would have no heir, both Louis XIV and Leopold I, Holy Roman Emperor, claimed the throne. Each had married sisters of Charles II. William III of England attempted to negotiate a diplomatic settlement for the Spanish succession that would bar the king of France and his family from the throne of

Spain. Charles II himself offered the crown of Spain to the younger grandson of Louis XIV in return for promises that the Bourbon would abandon any claims to the throne of France. The succession of Philip V, grandson of Louis XIV of France, brought on the War of the Spanish Succession in 1702. The Grand Alliance was renewed to confront the unified forces of Spain and France. The addition of Prussia to the Grand Alliance balanced the addition of Spain to the French royal house. Land battles generally favored the Grand Alliance, but no final military conclusion to the war was reached. The Peace of Utrecht ended the conflict by diplomatic compromise. The house of Bourbon remained in Spain and was recognized as the rightful ruling family. The emperor received the Spanish territories in Italy and the Spanish Netherlands.

D. The Colonial Wars

The Treaty of Utrecht, followed shortly thereafter by the death of Louis XIV, provided a temporary respite to the constant warfare. Emerging as the commercial leader in the aftermath of the wars was England. Key to England's commercial superiority was the development of North American colonies. The colonies provided ships, tobacco and sugar as exports. Equally important, the colonists were consumers of English manufactured goods. The English secured a monopoly of the slave trade with the Spanish colonies by the terms of the Treaty of Utrecht. England received small territories in the New World from France as well as Gibraltar in the Mediterranean. The major rival to England's dominance as the major commercial power in the world was France. Although France held the most profitable colony in the West Indies, its other colonies were not heavily settled by European immigrants. In contrast, the English colonies had, from the outset, attracted large numbers of settlers to the New World. In order to offset the population advantage held by the English, France sent armies to defend its North American colonies. When the English responded by sending military detachments to the western frontiers of the colonies, warfare ensued. The English turned the Seven Years' War into a contest for imperial domination. British navies extended the conflict from North America to the Caribbean sugar plantations and the merchant settlements of the Indian subcontinent. In all three theaters, the English were triumphant. In the Peace of Paris of 1763, France ceded its territories in North America in return for regaining the sugar islands of the Caribbean. British control of Indian trade was recognized.

TIMELINE

Insert the following events into the timeline. This should help you to compare important historical events chronologically.

end of Nine Years' War
trial of Galileo by Inquisition
end of Seven Years' War
beginning of War of Spanish Succession
Newton publishes *Mathematical Principles of Natural Philosophy*
Copernicus publishes *On the Revolution of the Heavenly Spheres*

1543	
1633	
1687	
1697	
1702	
1763	

TERMS, PEOPLE, EVENTS

The following terms, people, and events are important to your understanding of the chapter. Define each one.

Rembrandt van RiJn	scientific revolution	Nicolaus Copernicus
Tycho Brahe	Johannes Kepler	Galileo Galilei
Hermes Trismegistus	Paracelsus	alchemy
Robert Boyle	Andreas Vesalius	William Harvey
Sir Isaac Newton	Francis Bacon	Rene Descartes
Flyboats	triangular trade	giro banking
bills of exchange	Bank of England	calicoes
Mercantilism	monopoly	joint-stock companies
Navigation Acts	tariffs	Treaty of Nijmegen
balance of power	Nine Years' War	War of the Spanish Succession
Treaty of Utrecht	Seven Years' War	Peace of Paris
Cartesianism	entrepôt	Neoplanotnism

MAP EXERCISE

The following exercise is intended to clarify the geophysical environment and the spatial relationships among the important objects and places mentioned in the chapter.

1. Major contributions to the scientific revolution were made in all the locations listed bellow (in question number 2). What does this suggest about the rapid dissemination of knowledge during the scientific revolution? What contributed to the distribution of knowledge?

2. Locate the following places on the map.

    Krakow (Poland)   France
    Denmark   Padua
    England   Spanish Netherlands

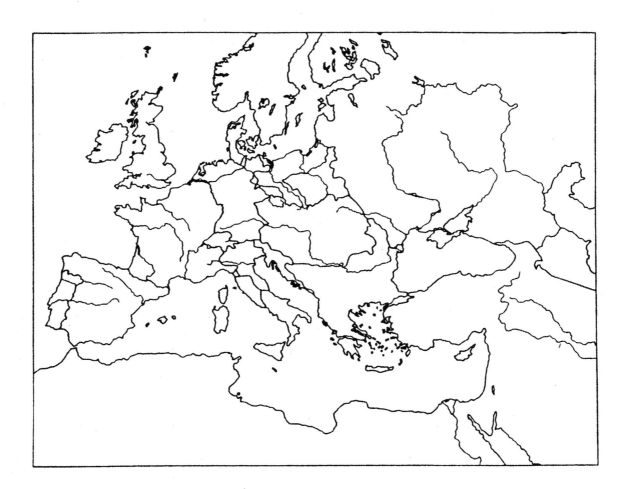

MAKING CONNECTIONS

The following questions are intended to emphasize important ideas within the chapter.

1. How did the new science differ from ancient science? What were the major astronomical, scientific, and mathematical discoveries?

2. Who tended to support the scientific revolution? Who opposed it? How did Descartes seek to establish a synthesis of the two positions?

3. What made possible the establishment of the European domination of international trade?

4. How did the establishment of worldwide trade networks affect the European consumption of goods?

5. What accounts for the temporary Dutch domination of worldwide trade?

6. Define mercantilism. What institutions were created by the European states to meet mercantile goals for economic development?

7. What were the imperial wars? Who was the overall victor?

PUTTING LARGER CONCEPTS TOGETHER

The following questions test your ability to summarize the major conclusions of the chapter.

1. In what ways did the European experiences of the seventeenth century mark a turning point in world civilizations? Consider both the scientific revolution and the European entry into worldwide commerce.

2. In what ways did the concept of the "balance of power" affect diplomacy and war in the late seventeenth and early eighteenth century?

SELF-TEST OF FACTUAL INFORMATION

1. The cosmos established by what ancient philosopher was overturned during the scientific revolution?

   a. Aristotle
   b. Plato
   c. Parmenides
   d. Thales

2. Which of the following statements concerning the astronomical discoveries of the scientific revolution is NOT accurate?

   a. Discoveries were made in virtually all parts of Europe.
   b. The Roman Catholic Church quickly accepted most of the findings.
   c. Monarchs and royal governments often patronized the astronomers and scientists.
   d. Galileo provided visual confirmation of the mathematical proofs offered by Johannes Kepler for a heliocentric universe.

3. The Swiss scientist Paracelsus

   a. rejected mysticism and Neoplatonism in his scientific experiments.
   b. discovered the secret of the body's circulatory system.
   c. concentrated on alchemy to unlock the essence of particular metals.
   d. taught that the world was composed of four elements—earth, water, fire, and air.

4. Newton's theory of gravity

   a. rejected in entirety the Hermetic writings.
   b. proposed that motion was the result of the interaction of objects and could be calculated mathematically.
   c. relied almost exclusively on the calculus developed by Leibniz.
   d. rejected the concept of materialism.

5. What philosopher attempted to harmonize the new science with religion?

   a. Paracelsus
   b. Vesalius
   c. Voltaire
   d. Descartes

6. Which of the following statements concerning the expansion of European trade in the seventeenth and eighteenth centuries is most accurate?

   a. It was dependent upon technological discoveries.
   b. The European discovery of new trade routes made possible their hegemony over worldwide commerce.
   c. There had never been a pattern of international trade prior to the European trade hegemony.
   d. Both the Mediterranean and Asian land trade routes began to decline in favor of direct oceanic commerce.

7. Which of the following business innovations was NOT developed in western Europe during the seventeenth and eighteenth centuries?

   a. giro banking
   b. double-entry bookkeeping
   c. triangular trade
   d. Bank of England

8. Which of the following was NOT part of the English triangular trade with the Americas and Africa?

   a. silk
   b. iron
   c. slaves
   d. sugar

9. Which of the following was NOT an aspect of mercantilism?

   a. monopolies
   b. tariffs
   c. Navigation Acts
   d. free trade

10. Which of the following statements concerning the Seven Years' War is NOT accurate?

    a. The war began when the British sent troops to clear the French from the Ohio River valley.
    b. The war was fought in India, America, and the European continent.
    c. The French emerged from the war with only their colonies in India intact.
    d. In the Peace of Paris the French ceded all of Canada to Britain.

CHAPTER 18

The Balance of Power in Eighteenth-Century Europe

OUTLINE

I. A Dashing Officer

From the mid-seventeenth century onward Britain was the leading sea-power as well as an important military power on land. Throughout the eighteenth century Britain successfully held French power in check.

II. A Grand Tour of Europe in 1714

A. Introduction

The treaties that ended the War of the Spanish Succession altered the political configurations of both western and eastern Europe. Continental rivalries were established that lasted for centuries.

B. Expansion of the Western Europe

Western European colonialism continued unchecked. Spanish and Portuguese colonies in Latin America continued to flourish despite weakness in the mother countries. Although Britain and France were both more powerful than either Spain or Portugal, they were unable to seize control of the Iberian colonies in the New World. France and England instead contested for colonial superiority in North America. France initially controlled Canada and the western portions of the continent from the Mississippi River valley to the Rocky Mountains. British settlements, more heavily populated than the French territories, were located along the Atlantic coast. In Asia and the Indian subcontinent the western European powers often settled for trading centers rather than imperial control. In the seventeenth century, however, some European states began to seize locations of valuable resources. The Dutch control of the Spice Islands, Ceylon, and parts of the Malay Peninsula was the most prominent colonial venture in Asia. Not all changes were colonial. England emerged as a great power. Joined with Scotland in 1707, Great Britain also had a dynastic change. The Stuart family ended with Queen Anne's death in 1714. The only available Protestant family with some relationship to the English throne was the house of Hanover, a line of German princes. By 1714 the United Provinces of the northern Netherlands had lost the economic vitality that had made them a European power. Eventually they lost their seaborne dominance to England and their control of continental trade to France. The southern portion of the Netherlands, the so-called Spanish Netherlands, was ceded to the Habsburgs of Austria as part of the peace settlement. France had expanded throughout the seventeenth century, at least in part due to the aggressive foreign policy of Louis XIV. At the outset of the eighteenth century, France was the most powerful of the western European states, but economically exhausted. Spain was the greatest loser of the western states. All of its far-flung continental empire had disappeared. Under the new Bourbon monarchs, the reduced Spain was able to recover some of its lost prosperity. Central Europe remained fragmented and decentralized under the loose authority of the Holy Roman or German Empire. Imperial control of the various principalities, bishoprics, and cities was nonexistent. The power of the Habsburg emperors was centered on the states of Austria, Bohemia, and Hungary. The Austrian Habsburgs, particularly Leopold I, successfully turned back the Ottoman threat to their domain and extended their control over the Spanish Netherlands, Naples, and the territory surrounding Milan in Italy. The remainder of Italy was divided among city-states and small kingdoms. Genoa and Venice were diminished in significance, but continued to exist as independent enclaves. In the center of the peninsula, the Papal States and the Grand Duchy of Tuscany were larger principalities. In the mountains of northwestern Italy, the Duchy of Savoy expanded its territories. In 1720, Victor Amadeus II of Savoy earned the title of king.

C. Realignment in Eastern Europe

The Treaty of Nystad of 1721 that ended the Great Northern War between Russia and Sweden set the boundaries of eastern Europe. Critical to political relationships were outlets to the sea, either the Baltic in the north or the Black Sea in the south. After the Great Northern War, Russia became the strongest power in the Baltic. Peter the Great celebrated his victory with the construction of the port city of Saint Petersburg. Sweden lost most of what Russia won. As the loser in the Great Northern War, Sweden ceded its Baltic possessions to Russia and its German ports to Hanover and Prussia. Sweden remained powerful only in Scandinavia. Brandenburg-Prussia became the most powerful state in northern Germany. In addition to its gains from Sweden, Brandenburg-Prussia also swallowed up smaller German neighbors. The greatest drawback for Brandenburg-Prussia was that a portion of Poland divided the two halves of the German state. Poland itself was one of the largest and weakest states in eastern Europe. Poland was seen by other states as largely defenseless.

III. The Rise of Russia

A. Introduction

Peter the Great revolutionized western European perceptions of Russia. Previously regarded as a crude and barbaric nation insignificant to the political affairs of western Europe, Russia emerged as a new power with the victory over the Swedes in 1721. The construction of a Russian navy threatened the maritime interests of western European powers. Peter also proclaimed himself emperor of all the Russias, adding a second imperial claim to the hierarchy of European monarchs.

B. The Reforms of Peter the Great

The process of militarization revolutionized not only Russian political administration but also the society. The poll tax, imposed as a means of raising money for the continuous war effort, recreated the Russian social structure. Mandatory military service affected both the rural gentry and the peasantry. The gentry's service was extended to include civil service after retirement from the military. In order to oversee the collection and distribution of the enormous resources devoted to the military, Peter created the Senate, a council of nine administrators. The Senate sent out the fiscals to investigate tax corruption and evasion. The tsar divided Russian society into three groups, military service, civil service, and those who owned landed estates in the Table of Ranks of 1722. Advancement through the ranks of each group was based on merit. To prepare men for military and civil service, Peter founded educational institutions for the military and for the liberal arts. Peter also attempted to westernize the Russian economy by increasing manufacturing. The state itself capitalized various industries. Peter's reforms alienated many of the old aristocracy. Peter believed that his own son, Alexis I, was implicated in the plots against the throne. Alexis' subsequent death threatened the political stability of Russia.

C. Life in Rural Russia

The Russian economy remained overwhelmingly rural and agricultural. Farming techniques were crude, and agricultural productivity was low. Between 1649 and the first quarter of the eighteenth century, Russian peasants progressively lost their freedom and became the property of those who owned the land on which the peasants worked. The serfs lived typically in small villages under the direction of landholders who were themselves subject to a crushing tax burden passed on to the peasants. Serfs and their land could be sold or otherwise disposed of at the whim of the landlord. State peasants worked on land owned by the state. Such agricultural laborers were liable to conscription for any state need— military, industrial, or agricultural. There was no effective resistance to serfdom. While large numbers did occasionally seek to flee the desperate conditions, most were simply enserfed elsewhere.

D. The Enlightened Empress Catherine

The fact that Russia survived the dynastic confusion after the death of Peter the Great was a testimony to the success of the former tsar's reforms. Population growth added to the prosperity of the landowners, who tended to reckon their wealth in terms of serfs. The nobility, created in return for service to the state, benefited from the weakness occasioned by the lack of an obvious dynastic heir to the throne. Life service to the state was reduced to a period of twenty-five years. Some sons were deferred from state service entirely. In 1762 all mandatory state service for the nobility was abolished. One of the most successful successors of Peter the Great was Catherine the Great. To the extent that it did not disturb the basis of Russian society, Catherine endorsed the western European philosophy of the Enlightenment. The tsarina attempted to reform the local government of Russia. Fifty districts were created to be governed by local landholders, now freed for local administrative duties due to the abolition of mandatory state service. Catherine also extended the educational reforms begun in the reign of Peter the Great. Elementary schools staffed by trained teachers brought education to the children of the nobility. Royal reforms did nothing to alter the desperate state of the Russian serfs. If anything, serfdom was expanded during Catherine's reign. Peasant dissatisfaction resulted in Pugachev's revolt, a rebellion of conscripted laborers and serfs. After more than a year of successes, Pugachev's army was defeated. The leader of the revolt, Emelyan Pugachev, was executed along with many of his followers.

IV. The Two Germanies

  A. Introduction

The Thirty Years' War devastated the Holy Roman Empire and left an already fragmented state divided into Austrian and German halves. In Germany, the larger principalities were essentially free of imperial interference. The most aggressive of these principalities was the kingdom of Prussia. The Habsburg estates of Austria, Bohemia, and Hungary remained the most powerful entities in the southern portions of the Holy Roman Empire.

  B. The Rise of Prussia

Successful participation in the War of the Spanish Succession and the Great Northern War converted the weak and fragmented holdings of Brandenburg into the powerful state of Brandenburg-Prussia. Under Frederick William I, all the resources of Brandenburg were dedicated to militarization. All citizens were liable to compulsory military service under the command of a local nobleman. Troops underwent military training during those seasons in which they were not needed as agricultural laborers. Despite the military build-up, Frederick William avoided lengthy wars in favor of administrative economy. Under his rule, Prussia's treasury enjoyed a surplus. The economies of Frederick William permitted the aggressive foreign policy of his son, Frederick the Great. Frederick took Silesia from Austria and plotted the seizure of the Polish corridor that divided Brandenburg from Prussia. Like his father, Frederick II built a centralized state based on military organization and a partnership with the Prussian nobility. Like Catherine the Great, Frederick endorsed the principles of the French Enlightenment and attempted to provide educational and legal reforms.

  C. Austria Survives

Although Austria emerged from the War of the Spanish Succession as the greatest winner in terms of the peace settlement, the Habsburgs suffered serious disadvantages. Many Protestants left the Habsburg territories for areas of greater toleration. The various Habsburg principalities Austria, Hungary, Bohemia, Italy, Naples, and the Spanish Netherlands differed in ethnic composition and felt little loyalty to the Habsburg confederation. As in Russia, the economy of Austria was largely agricultural and based on the labor of semi-free serfs. The Habsburg state was unable to tap the population effectively for military service. Most problematic was the lack of a male heir to the Habsburg dominions. In the Pragmatic Sanction, Charles VI named his daughter, Maria Theresa, as his heir. In order to secure the settlement, Charles was willing to grant concessions to the individual Habsburg principalities and to the other states of Europe. With total disregard for the Pragmatic Sanction, Frederick II of Prussia invaded Silesia immediately after the accession of Maria Theresa. Loss of Silesia prompted reform in Austria along the lines followed in Russia and Prussia. The government was centralized in order to streamline the collection of taxes to pay for a stronger military force. Maria Theresa and her son, Joseph II, worked to reduce the burdens of serfdom in the face of stern aristocratic resistance. In Austria and Bohemia, the reforms were largely successful. Hungary, however, attempted to preserve the local autonomy of the nobility.

D. The Politics of Power

Prussia's invasion of Silesia opened the door for other European states to launch an assault on the weakened Habsburg dominions. The result was the War of the Austrian Succession. France allied with Prussia; England and the Netherlands with Austria. The Peace of Aix-la-Chapelle of 1748 recognized Frederick's seizure of Silesia, but forced the French to withdraw again from the Netherlands. More than anything else, the war created an ongoing contest between Austria and Prussia for control of central Europe. In 1756 the alliances of the War of the Austrian Succession were virtually reversed. England supported Prussia, while France and Russia allied themselves with Austria. In the Seven Years' War, the Prussian armies were at first overwhelmed by the combined forces of Austria and Russia. Only the death of the Russian tsarina, Elizabeth, saved Frederick from total defeat. Subsequent dynastic confusion in Russia removed the eastern power from the war. Without Russian military support, Austria had little recourse but to conclude a peace. The war reinforced the rivalry between Prussia and Austria for mastery in central Europe. Peace, induced by exhaustion as much as by pacifism, followed the Seven Years' War. Of all the eastern states, only Poland remained immune to the reforms observable in Prussia, Russia, and Austria. The Polish monarchy remained elective so that no dynasty was able to solidify its hold on the administration. The Polish nobility remained largely unchecked. Unlike other eastern principalities, Poland remained largely defenseless. Given the obvious weakness of Poland, it was only a matter of time before the eastern powers discussed its division. Austria, Prussia, and Russia all actively participated in the partition of Poland. In 1772, Russia claimed the agricultural plains of northeastern Poland, Prussia took the Polish corridor that separated Brandenburg from Prussia, and Austria seized the province of Galicia.

V. The Greatness of Great Britain

A. Introduction

Great Britain was the greatest military and economic power of Europe by the middle of the eighteenth century. In Britain, unlike the powers of continental Europe, representative institutions and local elites shared authority with the monarch. The nature of the English constitution weakened central authority and allowed fragmentation into political factions.

B. The British Constitution

The British constitution balanced the interests of the monarchy, the aristocracy, and the commoners. The monarchy was not without power. As an institution, the monarchy remained popular with the people. The king also served as the head of the official Anglican church. The authority of the monarchy was, however, limited through the series of statutes enacted in the aftermath of the Glorious Revolution of 1688. The king could not suspend laws of the land. Monarchs were constrained to govern with Parliament through laws that required parliamentary consent for taxation and regular sessions of Parliament every seven years. The kings selected ministers and provided executive leadership within the administration. Parliament held the purse strings, made laws, and brought grievances to the attention of the royal administration. The balance of powers required all elements of the English constitution to work in partnership. Control of Parliament was difficult. There were 558 members of the House of Commons. Technically elected, most members of the lower house actually obtained their seats through nomination by the local elites within electoral districts. Actual political campaigns were uncommon. The gentry, familiar with the practice of local government, dominated the seats in the House of Commons. In background, the membership of the House of Commons differed little from the peers in the House of Lords. The Crown's management of Parliament depended on liberal use of political patronage and the distribution of royal appointments. These placemen formed the core of the court faction in Parliament.

C. Parties and Ministers

The techniques of parliamentary control developed more rapidly with the growth of political parties. The two earliest parties with origins in the late seventeenth century were the Whigs and the Tories. The latter supported the hereditary rights of the crown, but opposed the Catholicism of James II and participated in the Glorious Revolution of 1688. Subsequent support for the son of James II discredited the Tory party leadership. Whigs staunchly supported the Anglican church and the Hanoverian succession that followed the end of the Stuart dynasty. The association of the Whigs with the house of Hanover tied George I and George II to Whig party policies. The first great Whig party leader was Robert Walpole. From his position as First Lord of the Treasury, Walpole built an unassailable party leadership based on judicious distribution of patronage. At the heart of Walpole's policies was commitment to reduction of the public debt and to pursuit of the European balance of power. His inability to match his political aims with demands for war with Spain led to his downfall in 1741. The Whig ministers that followed Walpole continued to create a following by lavish gifts of patronage. Repeated use of patronage led to cries for reform.

D. America Revolts

The Seven Years' War brought England victory in the field, but a huge national debt. Parliament determined that the future cost of defending the North American colonies

50

should be borne by the colonists themselves. Parliament created new taxes in the colonies the Sugar Act and the Stamp Act to raise revenue for colonial defense. The American colonists overtly rejected the principle of taxation to raise revenue. Public violence directed at tax collectors broke out. Americans raised the issue of the unconstitutionality of taxation without direct representation in Parliament and questioned the need for a permanent British military force in North America. The British government stood on the principle of the sovereignty of Parliament to bind all British citizens to obedience. Americans picked up the cries for reform of Parliament and made use of English radical tactics use of the public press, boycotts of specific products, and public demonstrations. When the British government was unable to suppress the colonial movement, war ensued. After eight years of fighting, the colonists gained independence.

TIMELINE

Insert the following events into the timeline. This should help you to compare important historical events chronologically.

Peter the Great creates Table of Ranks
Succession of house of Hanover in Britain
Catherine the Great issues Charter of the Nobility

Beginning of Seven Years' War
Prussia invades Silesia
American Revolution begins

1714	
1722	
1740	
1756	
1775	
1786	

TERMS, PEOPLE, EVENTS

The following terms, people, and events are important to your understanding of the chapter. Define each one.

Peace of Utrecht
Peter the Great of Russia
Senate
Instruction
Frederick William I
MariaTheresa
Seven Years' War
placemen
Sir Robert Walpole
"emancipation of the nobility"

Treaty of Nystad
Brandenburg-Prussia
Table of Ranks
Charter of the Nobility
Frederick II the Great
Pragmatic Sanction
theory of mixed government
Whigs
George III
Table of ranks

Great Britain
Saint Petersburg
Stamp Act
Pugachev's revolt
Silesia
Joseph II
Sugar Act
Tories
Declaratory Act
War of the Austrian Succession

MAP EXERCISE

The following exercise is intended to clarify the geophysical environment and the spatial relationships among the important objects and places mentioned in the chapter.

1. Where were the most centralized states of Europe found by the end of the eighteenth century? Where was there a vacuum of centralized states? What accounts for this disparity?

2. Locate the following places on the map.

    Russian Empire   Brandenburg-Prussia
    Austria-Hungary   France
    Great Britain   Spain
    St. Petersburg   Sardinia
    Poland   Sweden

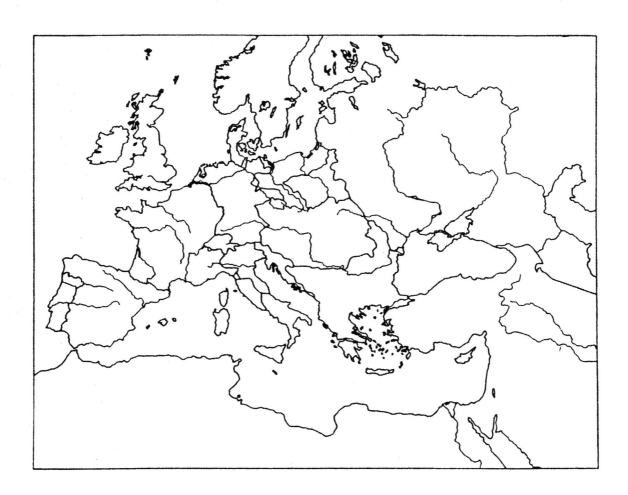

MAKING CONNECTIONS

The following questions are intended to emphasize important ideas within the chapter.

1. By 1714 what portions of the globe did western Europe control? How did their eastern colonies differ from their western colonies? How had the balance of power in western Europe changed?

2. How did the balance of power in eastern Europe change after the Treaty of Nystad?

3. What reforms did Peter the Great of Russia enact? How did they affect Russia?

4. What reforms did Catherine the Great of Russia enact? How did they affect Russia? What groups of Russian society benefited from the reforms? What group did not?

5. What reforms did Frederick William I of Prussia enact? What was his foreign policy? How did the foreign policy objectives of Frederick II the Great differ from his father's?

6. What innate problems did Austria face? What reforms did Maria Theresa and Joseph enact?

7. How did Britain's constitution differ from the other centralized states of Europe? What is meant by the "theory of mixed government"?

8. How was Robert Walpole able to establish himself as the first prime minister of Britain?

9. What was the nature of the debate between Britain and its North American colonies? What was the outcome of the debate?

PUTTING LARGER CONCEPTS TOGETHER

The following questions test your ability to summarize the major conclusions of the chapter.

1. In what ways were the reforms enacted in Prussia and Russia similar? What was their primary objective? In what ways did the methods of centralization differ? What different problems did these eastern European powers face? Which of the two powers was most successful in creating a centralized government? Why?

2. Compare and contrast the constitution of Britain to that of the eastern European powers. What accounts for the differences?

SELF-TEST OF FACTUAL INFORMATION

1. Which of the following did NOT cause changes in the boundaries of eighteenth-century Europe?

    a. imperial expansion
    b. incessant religious warfare
    c. nation/state mergers
    d. the contraction of Spain

2. The center of Europe in the eighteenth century could best be described as

    a. a cohesive religious and economic unit.
    b. an agglomeration of cities, bishoprics, principalities, and small states.
    c. the battlefield of two early modern superpowers the military giant of Prussia and the economic empire of Austria.
    d. the site of the most centralized states.

3. The Russian victory at Poltava

    a. won only temporary military advantage for the tsar.
    b. was made less significant by the lack of a Russian navy.
    c. forced the other states of Europe to regard Russia as a serious challenger in the struggle for diplomatic supremacy in Europe.
    d. resulted in the destruction of Prussian influence in eastern Europe.

4. The most important contribution Catherine the Great made early in her reign was the

    a. establishment of a legislative commission to review the laws of Russia.
    b. elimination of Russian Orthodox churchmen from state service.
    c. abolition of serfdom and establishment of a progressive form of sharecropping.
    d. peace pact she made with Sweden, thus ending sixty years of Russian humiliation.

5. Under Frederick William I, Prussia's foreign policy

    a. resulted in the seizure of Silesia.
    b. failed because of the lack of a sufficient military force.
    c. was largely pacific.
    d. was directed almost exclusively against Hanover.

6. Which of the following statements best describes Austria in the eighteenth century?

   a. It was a nation of shopkeepers concerned primarily with small-scale economic enterprise.
   b. It was a large, culturally unified federation with universal education and no taxation.
   c. The Austrian monarchy was a loose confederation of lands tied together by loyalty to a single ruler.
   d. An industrialized state, Austria was the leader in technical innovation and agricultural capitalism.

7. The Seven Years' War

   a. demonstrated that Prussia was NOT the military equal of Austria.
   b. initiated a long period of peace in eastern Europe.
   c. resulted in the overthrow of Frederick II the Great.
   d. resulted in the overthrow of Maria Theresa.

8. Which of the following nations did not join in the dismemberment of Poland in 1772?

   a. Russia
   b. France
   c. Prussia
   d. Austria

9. Which of the following statements concerning the British constitution is NOT accurate?

   a. The king continued to serve as the Supreme Head of the Anglican Church.
   b. Parliament consisted of three elements: monarch, lords, and commons.
   c. The king was charged with selecting ministers, initiating policy, and supervising administration.
   d. In the eighteenth century, Parliament established the right to impeach and depose the king.

10. Who was the first British prime minister?

   a. John Wilkes
   b. Robert Walpole
   c. Samuel Johnson
   d. John Churchill, Duke of Marlborough

Chapter 19

Culture and Society in Eighteenth-Century Europe

OUTLINE

I.   Happy Families

The concept of personal happiness as a desirable goal was a creation of the Enlightenment during the eighteenth century. Individuals and families measured their happiness as a reflection of the success of their societies. Yet as the wealthy pursued happiness through possessions and servants, the poor were often content with survival.

II.   Eighteenth-Century Culture

A. Introduction

The eighteenth century created a lavish and costly aristocratic culture. One of the most enduring results of this affluent culture was patronage of music. Noble patrons hired musicians and conductors, who were expected to cater to the whims of their aristocratic benefactors. When musicians proved too independent, as did Mozart, they failed to prosper. The literary and philosophical counterpart of musical patronage was the creation of urban salons, where influential thinkers exposed their ideas to an aristocratic audience and other members of the intellectual elite.

B. The Enlightenment

The Enlightenment reflected a set of attitudes critical of traditional European customs and morals. Those who adopted Enlightenment techniques of criticism were called *philosophes*. Although the Enlightenment began in France, its methods rapidly spread to the rest of Europe.

C. The Spirit of the Enlightenment

Three of the most important Enlightenment *philosophes* were Francois-Marie Arouet (called Voltaire) of France, David Hume of Scotland, and Charles-Louis de Secondat, Baron Montesquieu. In 1734 Voltaire, a French intellectual active in the salons of Paris, issued a laudatory editorial on English society entitled *Philosophical Letters Concerning the English Nation*. Its criticism of French society and the Roman Catholic Church stimulated an intellectual and philosophical revival that rapidly spread beyond the borders of France. In his early career, Voltaire was essentially a satirist of all traditional European culture—including the royalty. Exiled from France for his audacity, Voltaire traveled to England and remained there for two years. His praise of England in comparison to France caused the *philosophe* to retreat from Paris to the countryside. Following the death of his mistress, Voltaire traveled in Prussia and Switzerland— wearing out his welcome in both places. The end of his life was devoted to tireless assaults on Roman Catholicism in particular and religion in general. A university scholar, Hume spent most of his life as an author of philosophical treatises (largely unread during his lifetime) and histories (broadly popular). Hume was the ultimate skeptic who refused to accept the Cartesian synthesis and relegated all natural laws to the relativism of mental perception. He was, even during his own lifetime, renowned as an enemy of Christianity. Like Hume, Baron Montesquieu received university training. His most popular early work was *Persian Letters*, a satire of traditional European social organization and culture. Following a visit to Britain, Montesquieu undertook a comparative study of forms of government, *The Spirit of Laws*. In his work, Montesquieu advocated balanced constitutions as those most likely to maximize the pleasure of the governed. Enlightenment thinkers believed that the world could be reshaped by the proper application of scientific principles. Jean Jacques Rousseau and John Locke developed theories of education based on sense experience rather than moral indoctrination. Enlightenment thinkers such as Cesare Beccaria advocated social reform based on the concept of securing the greatest pleasure and the promotion of happiness. Some Enlightenment *philosophes* began to advocate the concept of progress based on reform and social evolution. Man was seen as a raw form capable of molding his society according to his personal experience. Mankind responded principally to pleasure and pain—one acted to maximize pleasure and reduce pain. According to the *philosophes*, the object of all governments should be "the greatest happiness of the greatest number." The Enlightenment world could not only be controlled, it could be managed for improvement. For the *philosophes*, progress was an identifiable goal.

D. The Impact of the Enlightenment

Intended for public consumption, it was inevitable that the Enlightenment would have some influence on European society. Curiously, political reform was embraced more willingly in eastern Europe than in the west. The three aspects of government most immediately affected were law, education, and the spread of religious toleration. In Austria, Prussia, and Russia, legal codification was undertaken, though not necessarily completed. As the Enlightenment thinkers commonly attacked the Jesuits, the religious order most associated with education in eastern Europe, the states had to create new educational institutions. Throughout the east, compulsory education programs were initiated. Religious toleration was readily granted in Austria, Prussia, and Russia. The strict regulation of minority sects was somewhat alleviated in western Europe, although general toleration did not exist in England, Spain, or France. Also influential were Enlightenment theories of economics. In France the physiocrats developed the theory that al wealth came from land, either directly or indirectly. State wealth should be based on taxation on the land. Physiocrats also proposed that the state should intervene as little as possible in private economic endeavor—the doctrine of laissez-faire. The ideas of the physiocrats and the Scottish intellectual Adam Smith provided the foundations for economic reform in the nineteenth century.

III. Eighteenth-Century Society

A. Introduction

Although eighteenth-century society remained highly stratified and hierarchical, it was inexorably altered by the emergence of the bourgeoisie.

B. The Nobility

At the pinnacle of society was the nobility. Those identified as aristocrats varied enormously in wealth, but the wealthiest members of the estate established the lifestyle to which all aspired. Wealth continued to be reckoned primarily in terms of the profit from ownership of land. The European aristocracy were consumers of luxury products and patrons of the arts. Their support of intellectuals and authors led to the Enlightenment as an expression of aristocratic culture. In all European countries the nobility was distinguished by degrees of privilege. It was common, however, for the aristocracy to be divided into the truly wealthy and those who simply held title but not necessarily wealth. The chief measure of noble wealth was possession of land, and aristocratic families devised various strategies to maintain their families' real property. In addition to land, nomination to national office often implied elevation to the nobility. Members of the aristocracy were supposed to engage in conspicuous consumption. They commonly spent huge sums on lavish palaces and country homes, grand tours of Europe, and patronage of the intellectuals. A universal aristocratic culture spawned a homogeneous European nobility.

C. The Bourgeoisie

Beneath the aristocracy were the bourgeoisie, the largely urban commercial class. Like the nobility, the bourgeoisie also developed a distinctive culture in the eighteenth century. At the center of bourgeois culture was the family and the home. Among the commercial classes, romantic love and paternal affection replaced the unemotional households of prior centuries.

The numbers of the bourgeoisie were greatest where the density of urbanization was greatest. The bourgeois percentage of the population varied from a high in the Netherlands to a low in Russia. The bourgeoisie was composed of various groups: wholesale merchants and international traders, retail shopkeepers, financiers, and professionals. As the pace of urbanization quickened during the eighteenth century, the number of the bourgeoisie multiplied. Mobility was characteristic of the various groups within the bourgeoisie. There was constant movement from the cities to rural estates in the countryside, as bourgeois families sought to move up the social ladder to the ranks of the nobility through the acquisition of real property.

Though they did not achieve solidarity as a class, the bourgeoisie did create a homogeneous culture. Merchants adopted more luxurious styles of dress, silverware, carriages and homes. Like the nobility, the bourgeoisie began to travel. In the case of the commercial classes, seaside resorts and baths were popular diversions. Greater wealth permitted more leisure. In response, theaters and music halls were developed to attract those with money and the time to spend it. By their purchase of tickets, the bourgeoisie became patrons of the arts. The expansion of the bourgeoisie led to greater literacy and the consequent rise in the number of cheaply printed books, newspapers, and magazines. The publications ran the gamut from light entertainment to serious political commentary.

Family life became the central feature of bourgeois culture. Prior to the eighteenth century family life was typified by a lack of affectional bonds between family members—between husband and wife, between parents and children. Families were patriarchal, and parental authority over children was based on beating. Under the Enlightenment encouragement for the pursuit of personal happiness, family life was transformed in the second half of the eighteenth century. Personal affection became a more common element of relationships between spouses. Domestic architecture permitted privacy for personal pursuits away from children and servants. Women typically bore fewer children, improving the quality of relationships between parents and children. Leisure and recreation became a normal part of childhood. The Enlightenment emphasis on education gave rise to the publication of didactic children's books. Increased wealth allowed both the leisure and money for parental investment in childhood education. Such advantages were not available to the working classes, where family life remained little changed.

D. The Masses

The poor of the eighteenth century shared few of the advantages of the nobility or the bourgeoisie. Despite the availability of greater supplies of food, additional housing, and more generous welfare, poverty was more prevalent than ever before—especially in the cities. Like the other classes, the poor did benefit from the establishment of a class culture that included a greater number of literate members of the working class than ever before.

The eighteenth century saw continuous and accelerating population growth unchecked by the sorts of demographic crises that had served to limit population in previous centuries. Thomas Malthus theorized that war, disease, and shortages in the food supply were natural, if tragic, controls on unlimited expansion of the population. In the sixteenth and seventeenth centuries, late marriages, clerical celibacy, and extraordinarily high death rates in the sprawling cities limited population growth. The eighteenth century reversed these trends. Women married at an earlier age, and the number of illegitimate births increased. As fertility rates improved, death rates fell. The plague made its last appearances in the seventeenth century. The impact of war was lessened. As a result, the number of people in Europe continuously grew after 1740.

An increase in agricultural productivity fueled the population increase. The problems of open-field agriculture were alleviated in the eighteenth century. New techniques included the voluntary enclosure of the open fields, introduction of fodder crops to replace fallow, and selective breeding in animal husbandry. New crops imported from the New World, such as corn and potatoes, offered new sources of nutrition. In many cases, the cause of increased agricultural productivity was simply an increase in the amount of acreage under cultivation. Particularly in eastern Europe, more land was brought into the agricultural system. Agriculture also responded to the upswing in the demand by creating a more efficient market. Farmers specialized in crops for distant markets rather than produce for local subsistence. It is also possible that the climate became warmer and wetter, thus creating a more hospitable environment for agricultural productivity.

As more people were born and survived the rigors of early childhood, the ranks of the impoverished swelled. Perhaps ten percent of the European population existed on the edge of starvation in complete poverty. Forty percent were essentially unemployed. The value of labor fell as the price of necessities such as food rose. Land was less available as more people sought to establish households. Poverty in the countryside forced those without access to land to emigrate to the cities, the frontiers of eastern Europe, or the New World. Squalor in the overcrowded ghettoes of eighteenth-century cities was appalling. No charities were able to stem the rising tide of misery. Hospitals were converted into holding pens for the indigent—the young, the old were crowded into conditions that guaranteed swift death. Crime soared in the cities, with the poor the most common victims.

Despite the overwhelming numbers of the poor, some among the working classes managed comfortable lifestyles. For those with some security and leisure, popular culture emerged to parallel the culture of the nobility and the bourgeoisie. Education increased literacy amongst the working classes. In response a market for popular literature in the guise of religious tracts, almanacs, serialized romances, and melodramatic tales of the Middle Ages emerged. More common recreation for the working classes consisted of festivals, sporting events, and blood sports. While the nobility had their salons and the bourgeoisie met in theaters, the working-class meeting place was the tavern.

TIMELINE

Insert the following events into the timeline. This should help you to compare important historical events chronologically.

Voltaire's *Philosophical Letters*   Rousseau's *The Social Contract*
Montesquieu's *Spirit of the Laws*   Malthus' *Essay on the Principles of Population*
first volume of the *Encyclopedia*   Locke's *An Essay Concerning Human Understanding*

1690	
1734	
1748	
1751	
1762	
1798	

TERMS, PEOPLE, EVENTS

The following terms, people, and events are important to your understanding of the chapter. Define each one.

Hidalgos	peerage	gentry
grandees	Jean Jacques Rousseau	Enlightenment
philosophes	*Encyclopedia*	Denis Diderot
Adam Smith	Cesare Beccaria	Immanuel Kant
Voltaire	David Hume	Montesquieu
Deists	John Locke	Fodder crops
Progress	religious toleration	physiocrats
market agriculture	bourgeoisie	petit bourgeois
domesticity	Thomas Malthus	"manure barrier"
laissez-faire	Salons	Patent of toleration

MAP EXERCISE

The following exercise is intended to clarify the geophysical environment and the spatial relationships among the important objects and places mentioned in the chapter.

1. How does the dissemination of Enlightenment ideas compare with that of the scientific revolution? [See Map Exercise in Chapter 17.]

2. What accounts for the rapid dissemination of Enlightenment ideas? Consider both technology and the state of Europe's diplomacy during this period.

3. Locate the following places on the map.

   a. In what country did the following philosophers work?

Diderot	Voltaire	Hume
Beccaria	Kant	Smith

   b. In which countries did monarchs attempt to impose reforms based on the Enlightenment?

   c. Where was the 1755 earthquake that deeply affected Voltaire?

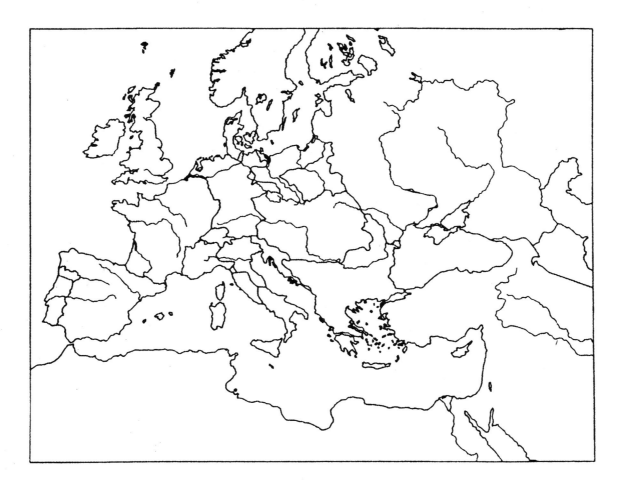

MAKING CONNECTIONS

The following questions are intended to emphasize important ideas within the chapter.

1. What were the contributions of Voltaire, Hume, and Montesquieu? How did these men reflect the general world view of the Enlightenment?

2. Why did the thinkers of the Enlightenment believe in optimism and progress?

3. What impact did the Enlightenment have on European governments? Where was this impact felt most completely?

4. Define, in so far as possible, the European nobility. In what ways did they differ from country to country?

5. Who were the bourgeoisie? What determined membership in this social classification?

6. What was the nature of bourgeois culture? How did the bourgeois family change?

7. What accounts for the great population increase of the eighteenth century? Why were changes in the agricultural system of Europe critical to population growth?

8. What accounts for the growing problem of poverty among the masses?

9. What was the nature of mass culture?

PUTTING LARGER CONCEPTS TOGETHER

The following questions test your ability to summarize the major conclusions of the chapter.

1. The rapid dissemination of Enlightenment ideas and culture resembles in many ways the rapid spread of the scientific revolution that preceded. In what ways was the Enlightenment similar? In what ways did it differ in fundamental assumptions and in the types of social questions it attempted to resolve?

2. How did the social system of the eighteenth century contrast with that of the sixteenth century? [See Chapter 15.] Were there any similarities?

SELF-TEST OF FACTUAL INFORMATION

1. Which of the following statements concerning the European nobility is most accurate?

    a. The nobility throughout Europe was an undifferentiated class.
    b. All who were truly wealthy were noble.
    c. All who were noble were wealthy.
    d. The nobility had ceased to play a role in national governments.

2. The collection that attempted to summarize all acquired knowledge was the

    a. *Almanach.*
    b. *Omnibus.*
    c. *Dictionaire.*
    d. *Encyclopedia.*

3. In government, Montesquieu advocated

    a. enlightened despotism.
    b. separation of powers.
    c. pure democracy.
    d. Plato's *Republic.*

4. What was the academic discipline of the French thinkers known as physiocrats?

    a. psychology
    b. economics
    c. theology
    d. chemistry

5. At the end of the eighteenth century, the European bourgeoisie

    a. was shrinking in size and economic importance.
    b. comprised less than twenty percent of the population, even in those states where they were most numerous.
    c. often lived in the countryside.
    d. comprised an undifferentiated class of wealthy financiers.

6. In the eighteenth century, improvements in food supply, housing, and sanitation led to

    a. a utopian existence for all.
    b. an end to social protests.
    c. more misery for the masses.
    d. an increased tax base for the state.

7. Which of the following was NOT an aspect of bourgeois culture?

    a. travel
    b. conspicuous consumption
    c. illiteracy
    d. theater and music halls

8. In which of the following ways did the bourgeois concept of family change?

    a. Changes in the construction of homes permitted married couples greater privacy and intimacy.
    b. The eighteenth-century family became matriarchal.
    c. Greater concern for family togetherness led to increasing numbers of children for bourgeois couples.
    d. Parents were less concerned over the care and education of children.

9. Where in Europe was there the greatest rate of population growth during the eighteenth century?

    a. Russia and Hungary
    b. England
    c. France, Spain, and Italy
    d. Prussia

10. Which of the following statements concerning mass culture is most accurate?

    a. The European poor, even in the most advanced countries, were almost entirely illiterate.
    b. The literate European masses were most attracted to melodramatic tales of knights and ladies from the age of chivalry.
    c. The rise of literacy brought an end to those community festivals that had characterized earlier periods of European life.
    d. The consumption of alcoholic beverages began to decrease during the eighteenth century.

Chapter 20

The French Revolution and the Napoleonic Era, 1789-1815

OUTLINE

I.   Eighteenth-Century Revolution

The late eighteenth century witnessed two separate revolutions. In America, the 13 British colonies attained their independence from England. In Europe, the French monarchy was toppled. The Two revolutions were influenced by the ideas of the eighteenth century *philosophes*.

II.   The Crisis of the Old Regime in France, 1715-1788

    A. Introduction

The French Revolution was an exciting and creative experiment in forms of government, political rights and social theories. The abolition of the absolute monarchy placed France on untested constitutional social grounds. The break with the past was chaotic and violent. Constitutional reform was accompanied by bloodshed and repression.

    B. The Political and Financial Crisis of Eighteenth Century France

France under Louis XV was in a constant state of financial crisis. The crisis was made worse by the huge debts contracted to finance the Seven Years' War. France's defeat left it financially exhausted and with a huge debt. The financial crisis increased tensions between the king and the aristocracy, particularly in the *parlements*, the courts of the French judicial system. Magistrates within the *parlements* began to refuse to publish royal decrees in an effort to hamstring the royal government. Louis XVI was heir to a divided kingdom deeply in debt. The new king made the situation worse by committing France to yet another costly war, the American Revolution. In desperation, Louis XVI agreed to call the Estates General in 1789 to deal with the fiscal crisis. The Estates General represented the three orders or estates of French Society—the clergy, the nobility and the commoners.

    C. Convening the Estates-General

The announcement of the elections set off rounds of political debate in all estates and classes. The Estates General provided a national forum for expressing public unhappiness to the government. The nobles were determined to preserve their social and economic status and increase their political role. The Third Estate used the public forum as a means of demanding a greater voice than that traditionally allotted to them. To regularize the registration of grievances, notebooks—*cahiers de doléances*—were carried by elected representatives to the Estates General. These collections of political dissatisfaction with the royal administration demonstrated the universality of unhappiness and the existence of a common political culture. The people of France, of all classes, were demanding a greater role in government.

The Estates General met in May, 1789. The representatives of the estates were separated in manner of dress and in location relative to the king. None of the estates could agree on the demands of the Third Estate for votes to be counted for each representative, rather than for each estate—a method that would swing the balance of power to the Third Estate. Under the influence of Abbe Emmanuel Joseph Sieyes, the Third Estate decided to meet apart from the other estates. Taking the name of the National Assembly and attracting reformers from the nobility and the clergy, the Third Estate met in a tennis court and proposed to construct a new French constitution. As the members of the Third Estate deliberated a new government for France, all the country awaited the results. Public frustration over the political stalemate and worsening economic conditions began to spark riots.

D. The outbreak of Revolutionary Action in 1789

Louis XVI refused to accept the existence of the National Assembly as a constitutional body. The king began to marshal troops at Versailles to enforce his will. In response, the citizens of Paris stormed the royal armory, a prison in Paris called the Bastille. The Parisian citizens took to arms and formed a citizen militia, the National Guard, in support of the National Assembly. Other cities and towns in France followed the lead of the Parisians, and national guards appeared throughout the country.

The peasantry, who continued to bear the brunt of taxation, regarded the creation of the National Guard in Paris and elsewhere as part of an aristocratic plot to frustrate reform. Desperate because of the disastrous condition of the agricultural economy, peasants began to revolt against the authority of the local aristocracy. When news of rural violence against aristocratic privilege reached the National Assembly, the representatives acted to restore order. Noble privilege was abolished, but peasants were expected to pay to escape from feudal labor services.

Women were active participants in all parts of the early stages of revolution. On 5 October 1789 a mob of Parisian women marched to Versailles to protest the soaring prices of food. Armed with pikes, the women routed the king's royal guards and killed several of them. Louis XVI was forced to return to Paris with the mob—a king taken prisoner by revolutionary women.

E. Declaring Political Rights

In late August of 1789 the national assembly issue Declaration of the Rights of Men and Citizen which enshrined the basic rights that all Frenchmen were entitled. The constitution of 1791 was the result of Enlightenment belief in the progress of mankind, but it was not democratic. Rights in property were retained, and only those who held property could vote. Those who controlled wealth were enshrined as the political elite in the 1791 constitution. In keeping with its enlightened philosophy, the new government abolished noble titles and guaranteed freedom of religion. For the length of the revolution, the French government even supported black liberation movements in the Caribbean and outlawed slavery. Women's rights were less well guarded, despite their seminal role in the revolution.

F. The Trials of Constitutional Monarchy

The National Assembly began the reconstruction of the French government by dividing the country into new administrative districts, *départements*. The first anniversary of the storming of the Bastille was converted into a national celebration of the revolution. The Roman Catholic Church also came under attack. All monasteries were dissolved, and priests became salaried employees of the state. Catholic clergy unwilling to take an oath to the National Assembly were driven into hiding. The assault on the Church created a meaningful counter-revolutionary movement among the aristocrats-in-exile, the émigrés. Finally, in 1791 the National Assembly issued a new constitution establishing a limited monarchy. Louis XVI, with little choice, accepted the new constitution. Within months, the king and his family attempted to flee the kingdom and join the counterrevolution. Captured by forces of the National Guard, the king was returned to Paris as a prisoner of the state. Other problems faced the new constitutional monarchy. By accepting the debts of the Old Regime, the new government began its existence hopelessly in arrears. To pay for its expenditures, the Assembly issued *assignats*, treasury bonds of dubious worth. Inflation ravaged the already depressed economy. Disgusted with the government's inability to control prices, peasants rioted throughout France. In the midst of economic disaster, the government declared war in 1792 on Austria.

IV. Experimenting with Democracy, 1792-1799

A. Introduction

As democracy began to replace monarchy in the French Revolution. It produced a new political universe populated by equal citizens instead of subjects of the king. All men, regardless of rank, were expected to participate in revolutionary politics. However, they were not experienced in the problems of exercising power.

B. The Revolution of the People

In 1792 the working classes of the cities radicalized the process of revolution. Craftsmen, called *sans-culottes*, took the movement toward democracy into their own hands. On 10 August 1792, the *sans-culottes* of Paris stormed the royal palace of the Tuileries.

C. "Terror is the Order of the Day"

The national Convention became fragmented into partisan political factions. The most radical members of the Convention—those who supported the movement of the *sans-culottes*—were Jacobins. The Girondins were a more moderate faction who supported the French war effort. As the Girondins were unable to control the mounting violence in the countryside and in the cities, the Jacobins were able to gain an advantage. In June 1793, a mob surrounded the Convention and effectively captured the Girondist members. The leader of the Jacobins was Maximilien Robespierre. He became head of the radical Committee of Public Safety, a twelve-man tribunal created to restore order in France. Robespierre and his allies began systematically to remove political rivals through mass executions—the so-called Reign of Terror. Every *departement* possessed its own guillotine for revolutionary justice. Even religion was democratized. Christianity was replaced by the cult of the supreme being, a religion of reason in a search for a new moral climate. As in the earlier stages of revolution, women were conspicuously absent from power. Women were deemed fit for domestic duties but not for political action. Eventually Robespierre and the Committee of Public Safety eliminated not only all rivals, but also all supporters. Without widespread public support, Robespierre fell in 1794 to the revolutionary justice he had established. With his execution, the Reign of Terror came to an end. The excesses of radical revolution cast both democracy and the *sans-culottes* into disfavor. Leadership in the revolution passed to more moderate forces.

D. The End of the Revolution

In the aftermath of Robespierre's fall, the government of France was controlled by the Directory, a committee of moderates who offered little more than stability. The greatest problem that confronted the Directory was the European war and its attendant costs. The reinstatement of conscription caused Frenchmen to look to other political leaders.

IV.   The Reign of Napoleon, 1799-1815

A. Introduction

Napoleon is a controversial historical figure. He attempted to construct a new government under his absolute rule but remained dedicated to the principles of the Enlightenment.

B. Bonaparte Seizes Power

Napoleon was born in Corsica and received an early military education. Without noble birth, his military career was truncated. The French Revolution eliminated many aristocratic commanders and made it possible for Bonaparte to establish a reputation for brilliance. In 1795 he crushed a Parisian revolt against the Directory. Immediately thereafter he enjoyed extraordinary victories in Syria, Egypt, and Italy. By 1799 he was sufficiently powerful to join a conspiracy against the Directory. The new government of which Napoleon was a member consisted of three consuls. As First Consul, Napoleon ended the de-Christianization campaign by signing the Concordat of 1801 with the Catholic church recognizing Catholicism as the religion of the French people. He also guaranteed the security of property taken during the revolution, thus eliminating the possibility of an aristocratic return to power. A plebiscite of 1802 rewarded the First Consul by granting him power for life.

C. Napoleon at War with the European Powers

The inevitable result of constant warfare was exhaustion. The first cracks in French military power appeared when it failed to crush Spanish guerillas in the Peninsular campaigns of 1808-1814. In 1812, the Napoleonic armies faltered during an ill-advised invasion of Russia. The armies of the tsar followed a scorched earth policy that left Napoleon's forces exposed to the cruelties of the Russian winter. The might of the French military was destroyed. All of France's former enemies rushed together to destroy the imperial forces in 1813 at the Battle of Nations near Leipzig. When allied forces took Paris, Napoleon abdicated and was exiled to the island of Elba. In 1815, the emperor escaped. In one last attempt, Napoleon faced the allied European nations at Waterloo only to be defeated for the final time. For a second time the emperor was exiled, this time to Saint Helena. He died there in 1821.

D. The First Empire and Domestic Reforms

In 1804 Napoleon had himself proclaimed emperor of France. He took the task of government seriously and began a series of reforms extending to almost every facet of life. The emperor reformed the disastrous tax system, created a central banking system, rebuilt the internal transportation network to facilitate trade, and emphasized the role of science in higher education. Most important, Napoleon required a new codification of French law. In the revolutionary tradition, women were reduced to a secondary legal status in the Napoleonic Codes.

E. Decline and Fall

The inevitable result of constant warfare was exhaustion. In 1812 the Napoleonic armies faltered during an ill-advised invasion of Russia. The armies of the tsar followed a scorched earth policy that left Napoleon's forces exposed to the cruelties of the Russian winter. The might of the French military was destroyed. All of France's former enemies rushed together to destroy the imperial forces in 1813 at the Battle of Nations near Leipzig. When allied forces took Paris, Napoleon abdicated and was exiled to the island of Elba. In 1815 the emperor escaped. In one last attempt, Napoleon faced the allied European nations at Waterloo only to be defeated for the final time. For a second time the emperor was exiled, this time to Saint Helena. He died there in 1821.

TIMELINE

Insert the following events into the timeline. This should help you to compare important historical events chronologically.

Napoleon proclaims himself emperor   creation of the First Republic
battle of Waterloo   Napoleon overthrows Directory
beginning of Reign of Terror   Third Estate declares itself National Assembly

1789	
1792	
1793	
1799	
1804	
1815	

TERMS, PEOPLE, EVENTS

The following terms, people, and events are important to your understanding of the chapter. Define each one.

ancien regime
Louis XVI
Peninsular War
Third Estate
Emmanuel Joseph Sieyes
Oath of the Tennis Court
National Guard
Constitution of 1791
sans-culottes
Jacobins
Committee of Public Safety
Thermidorian Reaction
First Consul
Charles Alexandre de Calonne
Civil Constitution of the Clergy

parlements
Jacques Necker
Estates General
French Revolution
Battle of Nations
Bastille
National Assembly
assignats
Convention
Girondins
Cult of the Supreme Being
Directory
Continental System
Conscription
Honore Gabriel Victor de
    Mirabeau

Lomenie de Brienne
Jacques Turgot
cahiers de doléances
Louis XV
Waterloo
Marquis de Lafayette
départements
Russian campaign of 1812
The Mountain
Maximilien Robespierre
Reign of Terror
Napoleon Bonaparte
Napoleonic Code
Old Regime

MAP EXERCISE

The following exercise is intended to clarify the geophysical environment and the spatial relationships among the important objects and places mentioned in the chapter.

1. How close did the Napoleonic Empire come to completing the French dream of continental dominance? Consider French foreign policy aims of Francis I and Louis XIV.

2. Locate the following places on the map.

    Identify all of those nations included within the French Empire established by Napoleon

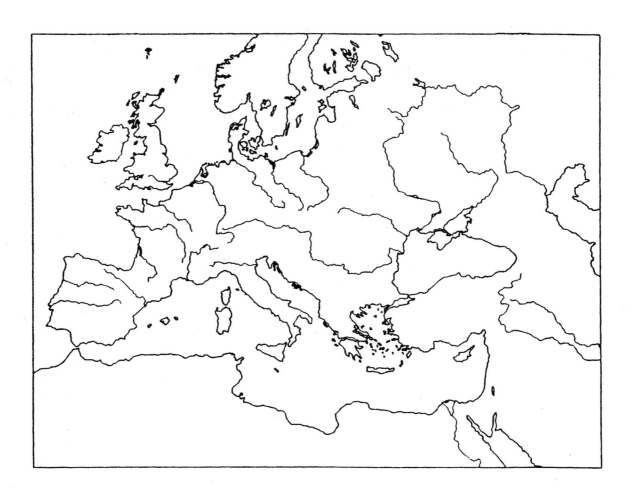

MAKING CONNECTIONS

The following questions are intended to emphasize important ideas within the chapter.

1. What were the causes for the collapse of the French *ancien regime*? Consider the reigns of both Louis XV and Louis XVI.

2. What was the social structure of France in 1789? How did the Third Estate seize the initiative in the earliest stage of the French Revolution?

3. How and why did the peasantry join the revolution? What contributions did women make?

4. What was the nature of the Constitution of 1791? Why did it fail to achieve permanence?

5. How was the social composition of the politically empowered revolutionaries changed after 1792? How did this affect the new constitution? How and why did the second stage of the French Revolution fail?

6. How did Napoleon Bonaparte seize control of the French Revolution? What sort of government did he establish?

7. What led to Napoleon's downfall?

PUTTING LARGER CONCEPTS TOGETHER

The following questions test your ability to summarize the major conclusions of the chapter.

1. Did the French Revolution succeed or fail? What were the objectives of the revolution at its outset? How were these modified throughout its progress? To what extent did Napoleon maintain revolutionary objectives? To what extent did Napoleon represent the antithesis of the revolutionary aims?

2. To what extent was the revolution in France an outcome of the social and economic reconfiguration of Europe during the eighteenth century? [See Chapter 19.] How successful was the revolution in creating new political forms to account for the new social structure of Europe?

SELF-TEST OF FACTUAL INFORMATION

1. Following the costly Seven Years' War, French magistrates attempted to stall increased taxation by

    a. arguing that the king had no right to invoke ship money taxes during peacetime.
    b. likening the king to a "fat cat" attempting to feast on the "mice", (the masses).
    c. comparing a tax increase with bleeding a sick man.
    d. charging the king with attacking liberty in his attempt to tax those who were exempt by virtue of their privileged status.

2. Prior to 1788, the Estates General of France last met in

    a. 1614.
    b. the reign of Louis XV.
    c. 1688.
    d. 1354.

3. Which of the following statements concerning the storming of the Bastille is MOST accurate?

    a. The leading characters in the violence were the poor, the unemployed, and the urban rabble.
    b. The popular resistance to the king represented by the assault lacked any formal leadership or organization.
    c. The purpose of the attack was to seize arms in order to prevent the royal army from suppressing the reform movement.
    d. The successful storming of the royal castle resulted in the seizure of the royal family.

4. The nationalization of Church property in 1789

    a. produced a national political consensus.
    b. caused the pope to denounce the principles of the revolution.
    c. bound the Catholic Church more closely to the process of revolution.
    d. reduced the likelihood of aristocratic counter-revolution.

5. What caused the Constitution of 1791 to lose credibility?

    a. The attempted flight of the royal family and the kings abandonment of the revolution.
    b. The Austrian and Prussian invasion of France.
    c. The English defeat of the revolutionary army at Toulon.
    d. The kings dismissal of the National Assembly.

6. The *sans-culottes* were

   a. disaffected nobles.
   b. the petite bourgeoisie.
   c. urban craftsmen.
   d. rural peasants.

7. The more radical political faction in France in 1793 was the

   a. Girondins.
   b. Plain.
   c. nobility.
   d. Jacobins.

8. Which of the following was NOT typical of the radical government during the Reign of Terror?

   a. women sharing in political power
   b. forty thousand executions
   c. massive military mobilization
   d. establishment of a secular religion of the state

9. Napoleon's most enduring achievement was

   a. the Napoleonic codification of laws.
   b. the establishment of revolutionary democracies throughout Europe.
   c. the conquest of England.
   d. the Continental System.

10. What military campaign shattered Napoleon's reputation for invincibility?

   a. Austerlitz
   b. Jena
   c. the invasion of Russia in 1812
   d. the Italian campaign

CHAPTER 21

Industrial Europe

OUTLINE

I.   An Iron Forge: Machinery and the Industrial Revolution

Industrialization replaced human and animal power with the machine. The New machines allowed one worker to do the work that before would have taken more than a hundred people.

II.   The Traditional Economy

A. Introduction

The traditional economy was labor-intensive agriculture. The great majority of Europeans remained farmers in the middle of the eighteenth century. By the 1700s the agricultural household had begun to supplement its income by accepting tasks associated with the production of cloth—particularly spinning and weaving. During the course of the nineteenth century the nature of the traditional economy was irrevocably changed.

B. Farming Families

Over much of Europe the land was still cultivated in the open-field system in the eighteenth century. The communal system of agricultural production was prolonged because of insufficient incentive for change, serfdom, and the dangers of experimentation. The traditional agricultural economy responded to the population growth of the mid-eighteenth century by opening more lands, often less fertile than those under cultivation. More intensive methods were required to increase productivity. The accelerated population growth after 1750 placed excessive strains on the land and the rural producers.

C. Rural Manufacture

Between 1700 and 1800 the European population increased by nearly 50 percent. The explosion of the population and the stress on the rural population opened the avenues for development of cottage industry. Capitalists provided raw wool or thread; rural households provided inexpensive labor. As landholdings grew smaller, the percentage of income derived from cottage industry became more significant to the rural poor and produced the putting-out system. Rural communities were organized to provide unskilled labor for the production of cloth. Capitalists supplied raw materials and sold the finished products. Little initial investment in machines was required, because most households already owned the required spinning wheels and looms. Eventually the percentage of income derived from rural industry became greater than that from agriculture for those families with little or no land. Because the wages for cottage industry were low, some rural poor who lost their association with the land became prisoners of the system. The traditional limits on new household formation through marriage that had operated in the exclusively agricultural society were removed. Indirectly, the establishment of the putting-out system fueled the increase of the population.

D. The Agricultural Revolution

Increase in agricultural productivity was achieved through intensified use of land already in production rather than through adding more acreage. Increasingly, commercial attitudes took over agricultural production. Wholesale enclosure and the end of the open-field system were the harbingers of the agricultural revolution. Though not always a peaceful process, the division of common lands into private farms permitted the development of a market-oriented agricultural economy. Instead of producing a broad range of crops, farmers tried to cultivate the one crop most likely to produce a profit. In England and Holland the agricultural revolution progressed most rapidly. Fodder crops such as clover and turnips were introduced to replace the fallow. Animal husbandry became vastly more important. In convertible husbandry, farmers switched closed fields between pasturage for animals and grain production in response to the price structure for specific commodities. The intensification of agricultural production fed the population explosion of the eighteenth and nineteenth centuries. In contrast, the destruction of communal agriculture left the rural poor without the traditional support structures of the open-field communities.

III. The Industrial Revolution in Britain

A. Introduction

Like the agricultural revolution, the Industrial Revolution in Britain irrevocably altered society. Machines replaced human and animal labor. The Industrial Revolution began a sustained period of economic growth between 1750 and 1850. As it progressed, England ceased to be an agricultural and rural society.

B. Britain First

Because it was first, Britain's Industrial Revolution is often used as a model of the process. All of the circumstances necessary for industrialization were present in Britain within a small geographical region. Because it was an island, Britain early developed a navy and consequently emerged as a leader in commerce and colonialism. Britain also possessed an enormous complex of navigable waterways—canals and rivers—that facilitated the rapid exchange of goods. Britain also had abundant mineral fuels, particularly coal. Coal replaced wood for domestic use and supplanted charcoal in the production of iron. In addition to natural resources, Britain had already developed a commercial infrastructure: foreign export markets, sources of raw materials, shipping, and banking. The Bank of England was created at the end of the seventeenth century to provide greater financial liquidity and to fund a national debt. Other banking enterprises on a more localized scale emerged along with the quickening pace of economic development. They were critical as a source of capital for investment.

C. Minerals and Metals

Without coal, there would have been no Industrial Revolution. The original investments in coal mining came from great landed families. The capital at first was utilized to solve fundamental technological problems of mining—how to extract coal from ever deeper seams. Extracting water from the pits, providing ventilation, and lifting the extracted coal were all impediments to deep mining. Newcomen's steam pump was critical in solving the various problems and replaced the labor of thousands. The invention permitted the widespread use of coal as an industrial fuel, particularly in the production of iron. Before coal, the individual industrial processes in the production of iron had to be located near supplies of wood. The use of coal as the smelting fuel was made possible by James Watt's invention of an improved steam engine. The new technology was applied at the foundries of John Wilkinson. The application of coal permitted other technological advances, including Cort's puddling and rolling processes. Iron output increased exponentially.

D. Cotton is King

The traditional English cloth industry was woolens, produced in the eighteenth century in the agricultural countryside by the putting-out system. As with mining, technological improvements revolutionized cloth production. The primary impediment to cloth manufacture was the lack of machinery for the production of thread. The spinning jenny, water frame, and Samuel Crompton's mule mechanized the process. Mechanization of cloth production led to the development of the factory system in which machines and the water power to run them were brought together with increasing numbers of unskilled laborers. Factories permitted strict supervision of the workforce and the division of labor into increasingly specialized activities. Concentration of labor moved the cloth industry out of the countryside and into the cities. Cotton cloth became the most important English manufactured product. Mechanization of cotton cloth, drove the handloom weaves out of work. In an attempt to maintain their position, groups of workers known as Luddites, engaged in machine breaking riots. They were quickly suppressed.

E. The Iron Horse

Increased production created a demand for improved systems of transportation. The emergence of the railway system was the technological response. The lapse of Watt's patent on the improved steam engine allowed other inventors to apply the machine to the problems of more rapid transportation. In 1830 the first commercial rail line was opened between Manchester and Liverpool, two industrial cities. The rail lines were an instant commercial success—even if the original investors failed to make a profit—and with governmental support, the railways rapidly spread throughout England. They spawned a demand for increasing amounts of iron and later steel that forced modernization of those related industries. Concepts of time and space were radically shortened as the railways brought people and goods closer together.

F   Entrepreneurs and Managers

The Industrial Revolution reorganized the relationship between capital and labor. Industrialists simultaneously increased output and lowered costs for manufactured goods. Successful entrepreneurs not only needed capital for investment, but also were required to closely supervise the development of their businesses, most particularly the organization of labor. Increasingly the processes of production were subdivided into more specific, basic tasks. In search of malleable workers at low cost, factory managers began to employ women and children. British entrepreneurs came from every social class in England—from the very poor to the very rich. Two different examples of successful English industrialists were Josiah Wedgwood and Robert Owen. Josiah Wedgwood, was an heir to a family pottery industry that he reconstructed along the lines of the factory system. The result was higher quality and greater output. He then was able to sell replicas of his quality pottery by the thousands. Robert Owen became a mill owner in New Lanark Scotland. Disgusted by the terrible working and moral conditions in the mill, he set out to ameliorate the conditions of labor in the factories.

G. The Wages of Progress

Robert Owen ended his life attempting to establish utopian communities for laborers. His efforts at last produced laws for improvement of working conditions for men and limited the sorts of labor imposed on women and children. By the middle of the nineteenth century, statutes addressing the health and working environment of laborers became more common. The Industrial Revolution caused basic shifts in the English population out of rural areas and into the manufacturing cities. By 1860 more than half of all Englishmen lived in towns. Early marriage and large families continued the surge in population. There is an ongoing debate concerning the benefits and losses of the Industrial Revolution. Per capita income increased demonstrably in the first half of the nineteenth century, but the increased wealth was not distributed evenly throughout society. Real wages for workers probably declined until about 1820, when conditions improved. Business cycles were more severe in an industrialized economy. The factory system destroyed the old domestic economy of the agricultural household when the individual replaced the family as the primary unit of production. Labor was more strictly controlled in the factories. Methods of payment required budgeting or starvation. The old society of estates was supplanted by the mid nineteenth century with a new social system of classes based on wealth and the relationship to the means of production.

IV. The Industrialization of the Continent

A. Introduction

Continental European leaders carefully studied Britain's Industrial Revolution as a model for economic development, but the development of industrialization on the Continent followed patterns dictated by local conditions. The technology of the revolution could be exported, but the conditions that called the inventions forth could not. The industrialization of the Continent was a slower process.

B. France: Industrialization Without Revolution

The industrialization of France was typified by slow growth keyed to local luxury demand rather than export markets. Two factors—population growth and the French Revolution—determined the nature of French industrialization. Famine and conscious limitation of family size restricted the rate of population growth in France. As a result, France did not experience the same pressures on the traditional agricultural economy as either Britain or Germany. The French Revolution was a disruptive force in the French economy. The commercial fleet was decimated. The urban guilds responsible for organization of crafts were abolished. The agricultural system fell into the hands of the peasantry who destroyed the open-field system but who did not have the capital for intensive improvements. The conservative agricultural system fed the population, but did not release large numbers of people to supply industrial labor. Until the nineteenth century, the French economy remained regionalized. The state was unable to create a centralized system through subsidies to national transportation networks or through development of banking schemes. Capital formation for investment was thus limited. Only in the mid-nineteenth century did the state finally initiate the construction of a national railroad network. Construction of railroads necessarily produced industrialization of the processes involved in the production of iron. Prohibitive tariff walls protected domestic French industries, which remained uncompetitive in international markets. There were some benefits to slow growth. French industrialization preserved the security of rural society. Urbanization proceeded without the severe problems encountered in the British Industrial Revolution.

C. Germany: Industrialization and Union

The political fragmentation of Germany retarded industrialization. Different currencies, regional tariffs, tolls and laws localized the economy. The traditional agricultural system continued in many parts of Central Europe. In the eastern states, serfdom still prevailed. In general, the peasantry became more free the farther west in Germany they were located. Even by 1800, eighty percent of the German population was engaged in agriculture. Germany also lacked a commercial foundation for industrialization. The Hanseatic cities had declined as international trade centers. The mechanization of German industries lagged far behind Britain into the middle of the nineteenth century. Prussia mounted the most successful attempt to overcome the impediments to industrialization. The government created a trade union, the *Zollverein*, composed of countries willing to adopt the lenient Prussian customs policies. The *Zollverein* was the first step in German political unification. Industrialization that followed the creation of the *Zollverein* was slavishly modeled after Britain. States invested heavily in the creation of railroads, particularly in Prussia. The Germans eventually developed proficient domestic centers of production for iron and engines.

D. The Lands That Time Forgot

The Netherlands, Austria, Russia, Spain, and the states of the Italian peninsula failed to develop industrial economies. Some lacked natural resources, others lacked transportation networks and the capital to produce them, and others were limited by geographical determinants (lack of waterways, mountains, etc.). All the countries that failed to industrialize featured traditional agricultural systems that were unable to increase their productivity to release surplus labor or to supply sufficient food to feed an industrial labor force. In some cases, serfdom was maintained with the active support of the state. Tariff systems protected inefficient local industries and isolated regional markets. In Austria-Hungary and Italy, some regions were favored for industrial development at the expense of others. Hungary, for example, was forced to retain a traditional agricultural system in order to foster the industrialization of Austria.

TIMELINE

Insert the following events into the timeline. This should help you to compare important historical events chronologically.

Watt's steam engine invented

Zollverein created in Prussia

first great canal opened in Britain

first modern railway opened in Britain

Factory Act in Britain prohibited child labor

Arkwright's water frame introduced

1760	
1769	
1775	
1830	
1833	
1834	

TERMS, PEOPLE, EVENTS

The following terms, people, and events are important to your understanding of the chapter. Define each one.

traditional economy

agricultural revolution

convertible husbandry

banking system

Henry Cort

John Kay

water frame

Samuel Crompton

Eli Whitney

Robert Owen

Zollverein

Crystal Palace exhibition

putting-out system

commercial agriculture

Industrial Revolution

Thomas Newcomen

puddling and rolling

James Hargreaves

Richard Arkwright

factories

George Stephenson

Edwin Chadwick

Friedrich Engels

Factory Act of 1833

entrepreneur

Charles Townshend

canal systems

James Watt

flying shuttle

jenny

mule

Luddites

Josiah Wedgwood

Great Hunger

Industrialization

MAP EXERCISE

The following exercise is intended to clarify the geophysical environment and the spatial relationships among the important objects and places mentioned in the chapter.

1. How are the elements of transportation, raw materials, and manufacturing centers related in Britain? What does this suggest about the necessary relationship among these variables in the process of industrialization?

2. Locate the following places on the map.

    major canals   major iron and coal deposits
    major industrial cities   major railroads

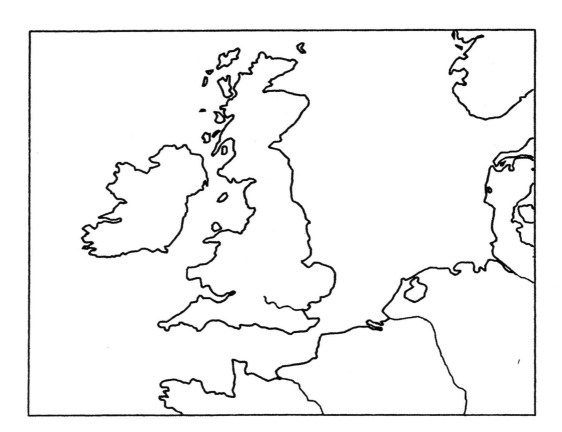

MAKING CONNECTIONS

The following questions are intended to emphasize important ideas within the chapter.

1. In what way was the traditional economy transformed by the putting-out system during the eighteenth century? What was the agricultural revolution?

2. What factors allowed Britain to undergo the first Industrial Revolution?

3. How did innovations in mining and metallurgy fuel the Industrial Revolution? What innovations in textiles led to industrialization?

4. What was the transport revolution? Why was it necessary?

5. In what way was the organization of business changed by the Industrial Revolution?

6. What were the social costs of industrialization? Did the costs outweigh the benefits?

7. What nations of continental Europe industrialized? How did their Industrial Revolutions compare to Britain's? What nations of Europe did not significantly industrialize? Why?

PUTTING LARGER CONCEPTS TOGETHER

The following questions test your ability to summarize the major conclusions of the chapter.

1. Industrialization was initially a British phenomenon. What factors facilitated industrialization? To what extent was the political environment of Britain significant? To what extent was Britain's emergence as the most powerful European nation a factor? How important were the Enlightenment concepts of free trade to industrialization?

2. Which of the above factors were less prevalent in Europe? Does this account for continental Europe's slower start? What other considerations slowed industrialization in parts of Europe?

SELF-TEST OF FACTUAL INFORMATION

1. The putting-out system

   a. required skilled labor to produce cloth.
   b. involved supplying raw materials to agricultural workers' homes for production.
   c. led to the development of the first rural factories.
   d. indirectly suppressed the growth of population.

2. One of the major features of the agricultural revolution was

   a. farming for the market rather than for subsistence.
   b. large-scale use of fertilizer.
   c. the use of metal-tipped plows.
   d. the open-field system.

3. Which of the following is NOT a reason that the Industrial Revolution occurred first in Britain?

   a. abundant mineral resources
   b. water resources and transportation
   c. effective infrastructure
   d. the largest population of European nations

4. Which of the following was NOT a technological innovation associated with mining and metallurgy?

   a. the water frame
   b. the steam pump
   c. use of coke
   d. rolling and puddling

5. The Luddites

   a. were responsible for the development of new processes for producing ceramics.
   b. organized machine-breaking riots in the 1810s.
   c. introduced the first efficient steam engine for railroads.
   d. invented the power looms that transformed the British textile industry.

6. The American inventor Eli Whitney was important to the British Industrial Revolution, because

   a. his development of steam-driven ships reduced the time needed to export goods.
   b. his cotton gin expanded American exports of raw cotton to feed the British textile industry.
   c. his reforms of the factory system revised the organization of business in Britain.
   d. his labor unions improved the working conditions of British laborers.

7. Industrial enterprises during the early stages of the Industrial Revolution

   a. were almost universally successful.
   b. were primarily family affairs with a high rate of failure as late as 1840.
   c. were exclusively dependent on capital provided by the state.
   d. failed to increase output or improve quality of goods.

8. Because the Continent industrialized later, it

   a. benefited from the example of Britain.
   b. lagged farther and farther behind Britain.
   c. could never make up the gap in development.
   d. became an economic colony of Britain.

9. Which of the following statements is most correct regarding French industrialization?

   a. France benefited from the most rapid population growth in Europe.
   b. France exploited a domestic market.
   c. The French Revolution clearly helped industrialization.
   d. France quickly outstripped Britain.

10. Why was the creation of an economic union critical to industrialization in Germany?

   a. It permitted exploitation of natural resources and construction of railroads.
   b. It added Austria to the German economy.
   c. It allowed Germany to depart from English models.
   d. It allowed widespread importation of foodstuffs.

CHAPTER 22

Social Transformations and Political Upheavals, 1815–1850

OUTLINE

I.   Potato Politics

In the eighteenth century, the potato was introduced to agricultural systems throughout Europe. In Ireland the potato became the exclusive staple and a substitute for wheat products in the diet. Between 1845 and 1850 a fungus decimated the potato crop, resulting in the Great Hunger. Millions of people perished or emigrated to the New World. Government intervention in the problems created by the failure of the potato crop proved unsuccessful, a harbinger of political complications caused by the increasing numbers of poor.

II. Geographical Tour: Europe In 1815

A. Introduction

The Napoleonic Wars created an independent European diplomatic system. The victorious states met in 1815 to create a stable European peace based on legitimacy, compensation, and balance of power.

B. The Congress of Vienna

The Four Powers of England, Austria, Prussia, and Russia determined the nature of the peace. In France the Bourbon monarchy was restored in the person of Louis XVIII, a brother of the slain Louis XVI. Treatment of the restored Bourbons was moderate. The allies then met at the Congress of Vienna to restore order to the rest of Europe. The object was to obtain a balance of power so that no country might dominate the diplomatic structure. Buffer kingdoms—the kingdom of the Netherlands and the kingdom of Sardinia—were created to contain France. The independent states of Italy were handed over to Austria. Even the Congress of Vienna could not remake the Holy Roman Empire. The German Confederation with its capital at Frankfurt consisted of Austria and thirty-eight smaller political units loosely bound together in a Federal Diet. Poland was a bone of contention between the eastern European powers, Russia and Prussia. After a series of secret negotiations, Poland was split between the two contenders. Prussia was also rewarded with other German territories and emerged as a contender with Austria for leadership in the new German Confederation. Of all the victorious allies, only Britain received no territorial advantages from the Congress of Vienna.

C. The Alliance System

To secure the settlements of the Congress of Vienna, two alliance systems emerged. The Quadruple Alliance (later the Quintuple Alliance after the addition of France) simply guaranteed the status quo in post-Napoleonic Europe. The Holy Alliance consisted of Austria, Prussia, and Russia and vowed to preserve peace and Christianity. England acted to offset the conservatism of the other allies. The English prime government refused to support intervention to replace constitutional governments with more conservative monarchies.

III.   The New Ideologies

A. Introduction

Industrialization changed the basic social structure of western Europe. Men began to identify themselves according to the new technology and the means of production. In response, new ideologies—liberalism, nationalism, romanticism, conservatism, and socialism—arose.

B. The New Politics of Preserving Order

Governments sought to establish a balance between state authority and individual liberty while preserving political stability. Conservatives stressed tradition and the necessity of corporate institutions. They valued slow evolution rather than traumatic revolutionary change. Politically, conservatives argued for the retention of monarchy. Under the leadership of the Austrian minister, Klemens von Metternich, conservatism took a reactionary turn. In eastern Europe, governments attempted to snuff out all constitutional reform or attempts to improve civil liberties.

Liberalism was based on two fundamental tenets: the freedom of the individual and the corruptibility of authority. Liberals embraced constitutional monarchy and the withdrawal of the government from intervention in private action. Liberals could be found in post-revolutionary France and in Great Britain. David Ricardo argued that government interference in setting wages only guaranteed the continuation of subsistence-level pay for the working class. Jeremy Bentham, another British liberal, created a social philosophy called utilitarianism. Governments could measure the benefits of their actions in the pursuit of social harmony while retaining protection of individual rights. James Mill embraced Bentham's philosophy. Mill's son, John Stuart Mill, however, rejected utilitarianism in favor of a more active social program. He argued for a more equitable distribution of wealth and for women's equality.

C. Romanticism and Change

Romanticism as a movement encapsulated a group of artistic and literary styles that tended to correspond to the political ideologies of the day. Among the founders of romantic poetry were William Wordsworth and Samuel Taylor Coleridge. At the root of romanticism was an emphasis on emotion rather than intellect. Even in gardening, romantics rejected classical formalism in favor of the "natural." Romantics embraced the concept of the inspired artist who created on the basis of the spirit rather than his understanding of classical models of color and balance. Representative of the French school of romanticism were Germaine de Stael and Victor Hugo. Both emphasized the necessity of subjective self-consciousness. Musicians, too, celebrated national heritages. Hector Berlioz, Frederic Chopin, and Franz Liszt incorporated the melodies of their native homelands into their compositions. Artists experimented with new colorations and compositions outside classical traditions. Romanticism embodied rebellion from authority.

D. Reshaping State and Society

Nationalism and liberalism, particularly on the Continent, were frequently interwoven political doctrines. Nationalism emerged from the desire to create constitutional governments free of tyranny and foreign domination. Nationalists sought to capture the national spirit in literature, art, or music. Frenchmen glorified the Revolution. Germans stressed a German folk culture as the source of national identity. The Italian Giuseppe Mazzini organized Young Italy for the purpose of unifying Italy under a republican government of Italian nationals. Germany also had a strong nationalist movement seeking to create a united German state. Georg Friedrich List rejected liberal economic theories and argued for a strong tariff system to protect and develop German industries.

Socialism was the political creation of industrialization. In the theories of the French utopian, Henri, Comte de Saint-Simon, industrialized society could be organized according to the hierarchy of productive work. Pierre Joseph Proudhon radicalized Saint-Simon's industrialized society by arguing that people had the right only to that property that was the result of their labor. Capitalists, who profited from the labor of others, were not entitled to property. Another utopian, Charles Fourier, urged the formation of laboring groups called phalansteries. Members of *phalansteries* were mutually responsible for the welfare of the group. Work was distributed evenly and strictly limited. Curiously, Fourier's phalansteries, the creation of industrialized society, were always rural. Socialist utopians differed in their approach to the position of women in society. While the socialist utopians hoped for peaceful social change, some socialists presented a revolutionary agenda for action. Karl Marx and Friedrich Engels proposed that the growing distance between the capitalists and the working class would lead inevitably to class struggle. Their theories were presented in *The Communist Manifesto*.

IV. Protest and Revolution

A. Introduction

The radical changes experienced by European society in the early nineteenth century created new sources of exploitation and misery.

B. Causes of Social Instability

Internal immigration from the rural countryside to the cities accounted for a significant urbanization of Europe. Migrants frequently took up unskilled jobs at low pay. The situation was more desperate for women, who at times were forced into prostitution. Venereal disease became epidemic. Urban centers spawned surges in crime. In response, some cities formed police forces to suppress the criminal element. Crime was often associated with poverty as a social issue.

Provisions for the poor—whether deserving poor or the simply unemployed—became part of the legislation that states created to deal with the problems associated with industrialization. Various approaches to poverty were proposed. Some argued that disease and famine were necessary correctives to overpopulation and that governments should allow "natural" measures to take their course. Others felt that the state had aided in the creation of the new society and therefore should play a positive role in curing its ills. In Britain, Parliament issued a series of statutes aimed at resolving some of the worst abuses of industrialization: exploitation of women and child laborers. Legislation shortened working hours and improved working conditions in the factories.

C. The Revolutions of 1830

Governmental failure to deal with harvest failures touched off revolutions in 1830. In France, Charles X attempted to restore conservative monarchy based on the old alliance with Roman Catholicism. The opposition to the reimposition of the Old Regime came primarily from bourgeois critics seeking a continuing liberalization of the constitution. As food prices rose, people took to the streets in Paris. Disorder and public disaffection with the government rapidly spread to other areas in France. Charles X abdicated. The urban revolutionaries urged the creation of a republic, but the politically empowered bourgeoisie established a constitutional monarchy, the so-called July Monarchy. The new constitution retained the political monopoly of the bourgeoisie.

In Britain, Germany, and Switzerland, rising food prices led to disturbances but not revolutions. Revolution against the Ottoman Empire's overlordship broke out in Greece in the 1820s. Finally in 1827 England, Russia, and France agreed to support the cause of Greek independence, if only to restore stability to the region. Defeat of an Ottoman fleet achieved Greek separation from the Turks. Belgium also sought to gain its independence from the kingdom of the Netherlands on the basis of religious freedom and economic prosperity. Although the eastern monarchs wanted to crush the rebellion, England and France refused. In the end, a constitutional monarchy was established in Belgium on the condition that the new nation maintain political neutrality. Poland, partitioned on several occasions and occupied by both German and Russian overlords, also revolted to secure independence. When peasantry and landlords were unable to cooperate, the revolution was resolutely crushed. Polish nationalism and liberalism continued to exist only among exiles. Revolution also failed in Italy where the states of Modena and Parma attempted to free themselves from Habsburg Austria. Young Italy, Mazzini's underground nationalist movement, continued to operate. The revolutions of 1830 demonstrated the continued vitality of the interlocking diplomatic system established at the Congress of Vienna. Great powers either crushed rebellions or compromised with mutual agreements for the establishment of new states. Maintaining internal stability was critical to the diplomatic balance of power. Finally, the revolutions of 1830 demonstrated a growing political consciousness among the working classes.

D. Reform In Great Britain

The English electoral system was unchanged since the Middle Ages. It did not reflect the social changes of industrialization. Urban areas were under-represented. Capitalists were hardly represented at all. The Reform Bill of 1832 extended the franchise to the industrial and commercial elite. The Reform Bill of 1832 did nothing for the working classes, who initiated a new reform movement summarized in the People's Charter. The charter called for universal male suffrage, paid parliamentary representatives, the secret ballot, equal electoral districts, and annual elections. Chartism was popular among the working classes, particularly ethnic minorities in urban areas. Poor harvests led to periods of Chartist unrest and labor strikes that always stopped just short of violence. In 1848 a huge mob carried a petition in favor of the charter to Parliament. Despite the popularity of the charter, the English legislature refused further reforms and the movement withered away.

E. Workers Unite

The technological mechanization of manufacturing was greeted by dismay and occasional violence by skilled labor. Craft workers banded together to prevent the erosion of skilled labor. Opposition to mechanization of production led to outbreaks of violence and machine breaking in England, France, and Germany. The English movement against machines was called Luddism. In England craftsmen tended to support the charter; in France they turned to riots and strikes during the 1830s. More radical members of the crafts turned to socialism and republicanism. Skilled craftsmen opposed women in the workforce, as female labor was inexpensive, unskilled, and "sweated." Women labor leaders, such as Flora Tristan, argued that the only hope of equality with males lay in education and organization. Generally, however, women remained outside the labor movement.

F. Revolutions Across Europe, 1848-1850

Revolutions swept all of continental Europe in 1848. As was common, poor harvests and rising food prices preceded political violence. At the same time, working class agitation for reform of political systems became more widespread. Finally many ethnic groups in Europe began to demand political boundaries more consonant with ethnic homogeneity. In France the revolution of 1848 broke out between Parisian laborers and the bourgeois government of the July Monarchy. The militia, the National Guard, joined the revolution as did some of the army. Like his Bourbon predecessor, Louis Philippe abdicated. An uneasy coalition of revolutionaries under Alphonse de Lamartine formed an interim government, the Provisional Government of the Second Republic. To placate revolutionary laborers, the government set up national workshops that soon deteriorated into an inefficient program of public charity for the unemployed. When the workshops drew the jobless from all over France to Paris, the government abandoned them and attempted to suppress the working-class element of the revolution. Armies under General Cavaignac crushed an abortive revolt of craftsmen and laborers.

Demands for ethnic solidarity and constitutional reforms were repeated in all the German states, including Prussia and Austria. Even the Prussian monarch was forced to accede to the creation of a new constitution. Demands for German unity led to the formation of a Pan-Germanic conference at Frankfurt in 1848 to design a new German nation. Debate emerged over the wisdom of including the maximum area within the new nation, including non-German ethnic minorities, or restricting the new nation to a smaller region that would be predominantly German. In 1849 the Frankfurt meeting chose the small Germany option. The movement failed when Frederick William IV refused to accept the crown of the newly formed nation.

In Austria, revolution broke out in the capital of Vienna and in Budapest and Prague. Revolutions were led in these cities by German, Magyar, and Czech nationalists, respectively. Metternich resigned in the face of demands for constitutional reform.

Outside Austria, Italian revolutionaries renewed their demands for independence from Austria. Temporarily, Giuseppe Mazzini established a republic in Rome. The revolutionary government withered away before the assault of French troops sent to restore papal rule in Rome. Similarly, each of the revolutions in the Austrian homeland were defeated in the course of 1849. Austria forced Prussia to forego any plans for a unified Germany. Conservatism was maintained by military force.

The revolutions of 1848 weakened the political balance reached in the Congress of Vienna. Austria only barely survived the challenge to the status quo. Failure of the revolutions was due more to the inability of bourgeois liberals and working-class democrats to coordinate their efforts. The victors of the revolutions of 1848 were generally the middle class. Ignored were demands for national entities based on homogeneous ethnic populations. Democracy was not achieved anywhere. The revolutions of 1848 had few concrete results.

TIMELINE

Insert the following events into the timeline. This should help you to compare important historical events chronologically.

Frankfurt parliament   creation of July Monarchy in France
Peterloo Massacre   Britain's Great Reform Bill
restoration of Bourbon monarchy in Spain   end of Congress of Vienna

1815	
1819	
1823	
1830	
1832	
1848	

TERMS, PEOPLE, EVENTS

The following terms, people, and events are important to your understanding of the chapter. Define each one.

potato famine
Viscount Castlereagh
Frederick William III
Holy Alliance
liberalism
nationalism
romanticism
Johann Wolfgang von Goethe
socialism
Charles Fourier
July Monarchy
rotten boroughs
proletariat
Louis Blanc
Louis Cavaignac
The Communist Manifesto

Congress of Vienna
Alexander I
German Confederation
Jane Austen
Jeremy Bentham
Giuseppe Mazzini
Germaine de Stael
Carlsbad decrees
Henri de Saint-Simon
Peterloo Massacre
Louis Philippe
1832 Reform Bill
Second Republic
Luxembourg Commission
Frankfurt parliament
Chartism

Klemens von Metternich
Lajos Kossuth
Quadruple Alliance
Queen Victoria
utilitarianism
Georg Friedrich List
humiliation of Olmutz
conservatism
Pierre Joseph Proudhon
Charles X
Young Italy
People's Charter
Alphonse de Lamartine
national workshops
Charles Maurice de Talleyrand
Proletariat

MAP EXERCISE

The following exercise is intended to clarify the geophysical environment and the spatial relationships among the important objects and places mentioned in the chapter.

1. Considering all the revolutions between 1830 and 1848, what part of Europe was most prone to revolutionary violence? What parts of Europe escaped revolutionary violence? What parts of Europe experienced permanent changes of government?

2. Locate the following places on the map.

    Mark nations with revolutions in 1830 with a "30."
    Mark nations with revolutions in 1848 with a "48. "
    Mark those nations with permanent changes of government with an "x."

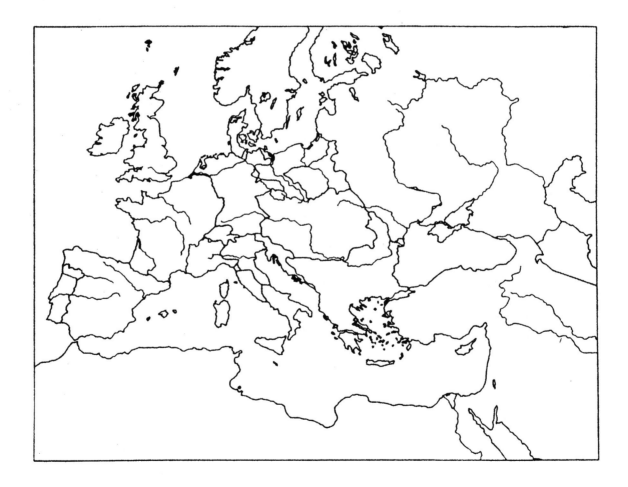

MAKING CONNECTIONS

The following questions are intended to emphasize important ideas within the chapter.

1.   What was the primary objective of the Congress of Vienna? How was it realized? How did the alliance system fit into the objectives?

2.   How did European society change after 1815? How did states attempt to meet social challenges? In what way did family structures change?

3.   What were the new political and intellectual currents of the nineteenth century? How were these new ideas related to the new Europe established by the Congress of Vienna?

4.   What was the result of the revolutions of 1830?

5.   Why was reform necessary in Britain in the nineteenth century? How successful was the reform movement?

6.   Where did revolutions break out in 1848? What was the result of these revolutions?

7.   What was the source of tension in Europe in 1850? How was it related to the failure of the revolutions of 1848?

PUTTING LARGER CONCEPTS TOGETHER

The following questions test your ability to summarize the major conclusions of the chapter.

1.   What accounts for the prominence of central Europe in the revolutionary movements between 1830 and 1848?

2.   Considering the political history of Europe from 1815 to 1870, how successful was the Congress of Vienna in establishing stability? Hint: What permanent changes took place in European governments during this period?

SELF-TEST OF FACTUAL INFORMATION

1. Which of the following was NOT a result of the devastation of the Irish potato crop beginning in 1845?

    a. A million Irish people emigrated, many to the United States.
    b. Famine and disease killed more than one million people.
    c. The crisis was relieved by successful programs initiated by the government of the United Kingdom.
    d. The Irish population was reduced by 25 percent in five years.

2. What was the primary objective of the diplomats at the Congress of Vienna?

    a. restoration of a united Poland
    b. the achievement of political and territorial stability
    c. the punishment of France for Napoleon's conquests
    d. the recognition of a united Germany

3. The two main tenets that underlay nineteenth-century liberalism were

    a. democracy and a state-controlled economy.
    b. maintenance of the status quo and abandonment of reform.
    c. abolition of monarchy and support for democracy.
    d. freedom of the individual and corruptibility of authority.

4. Nationalism was often associated with

    a. conservatism.
    b. socialism.
    c. liberalism.
    d. utopianism.

5. The person often hailed as the founder of French romanticism was

    a. Voltaire.
    b. Germaine de Stael.
    c. Antoine Lavoisier.
    d. Madame Roland.

6. The French revolution of 1830 resulted in

    a. the solidification of the reign of Charles X.
    b. the July Monarchy.
    c. the election of the Third Republic.
    d. the creation of the Second Empire.

7. Which of the following was NOT part of the People's Charter?

    a. the secret ballot
    b. universal male suffrage
    c. equal electoral districts
    d. equal political and economic rights for women

8. During 1848, revolutions broke out in all the following nations EXCEPT

    a. France.
    b. Belgium.
    c. Italy.
    d. Hungary.

9. Which of the following statements best explains the failure of the Frankfurt parliament in 1848?

    a. The parliament opted for a "large Germany."
    b. Non-German minorities in German states and Germans living outside Germany complicated any agreement.
    c. Frederick William IV was unacceptable to most Germans.
    d. Lajos Kossuth ejected the parliament before it could reach its conclusion.

10. As a result of the revolutions of 1848

    a. Austria collapsed into its constituent monarchies.
    b. Italy gained independence.
    c. the concert of Europe defined in the Congress of Vienna came to an end.
    d. France established a permanent democracy.

Chapter 23

State-Building and Social Change in Europe, 1850–1871

OUTLINE

I.   The Birth of the German Empire

The Princes of the German states and the military class of Prussia met at Louis XIV's splendid palace of Versailles to celebrate the creation of a unified Germany in 1871. The creation of the Second Reich was a military achievement orchestrated by Otto von Bismarck in the name of the king of Prussia, Wilhelm I. The German empire was the offspring of the marriage of "iron and blood."

II.   Building Nations: The Politics of Unification

    A. Introduction

The liberal revolutions of 1848 failed to procure change. In their aftermath, powerful politicians crafted new centralized states to replace the weakened survivors of the Congress of Vienna. Reform came from within the new states, not from the unempowered revolutionary masses.

    B. The Crimean War

Russian foreign policy was dedicated to acquiring a warm water port in the Mediterranean. In order to do so, the Russians needed to benefit from the collapse of the Ottoman Empire. After the Turks refused to recognize Russia's claims to protect Greek Orthodox citizens of the Ottoman Empire, the tsar ordered troops into the Balkans. The Turks then declared war. Although the Russians were able to defeat the Turks without difficulty, their victory aroused the concern of the French and British who also had interests in the eastern Mediterranean. In 1854 the western European powers declared war on Russia, as did the Italian kingdom of Sardinia. The resulting conflict was the Crimean War. The Russians eventually conceded defeat and surrendered their claims within the Ottoman Empire. The Danubian Principalities that had been the original focus of Russian interests were combined into the new nation of Romania. The war was a monument to military incompetence and brutality, but it destabilized eastern Europe by causing the Russians to withdraw from the balance of power. The Concert of Europe had ended.

    C. Unifying Italy

Italian unification failed in 1848. In the 1850s leadership in the Risorgimento fell to Camillo di Cavour, premier of Sardinia. Cavour began by liberal reforms within Sardinia and created an image of modern progressivism. He also brought the French into an alliance against the Austrian overlords of Italy. In the war that followed Cavour's diplomatic maneuvers, Austria's defeat delivered Lombardy to the kingdom of Sardinia. Other small northern Italian states were added through plebiscites. Central Italy followed in the same fashion. Under the leadership of Giuseppe Garibaldi and his Thousand Red Shirts, the king of Sicily was overthrown. Cavour also invaded southern Italy, leading to the declaration of a united Italy under Victor Emmanuel II in 1861. By 1870 Victor Emmanuel also gained control of Rome and Venetia, completing the unification of the Italian peninsula.

D. Unifying Germany

Otto von Bismarck was the architect of German unity in the name of preserving the leadership of Prussia. He invented the practice of *realpolitik*, pursuit of national interests at all costs. Bismarck's talent was his ability to join the conservative Junkers with the liberals in the pursuit of a united Germany. He utilized the *Zollverein* to isolate Austria economically, reorganized the Prussian army, and created a crisis between Austria and Prussia over management of the newly conquered territories of Schleswig and Holstein. In the Seven Weeks' War, Bismarck's new military forces destroyed the myth of Austrian dominance in central Europe. Austria withdrew from the emerging Germany. The Habsburg Empire divided itself into a dual monarchy—Austria-Hungary—under a single Habsburg ruler. With Austria removed as a potential rival, Bismarck was free to pressure the fragmented states of southern Germany into accepting Prussian leadership. French resistance to further gains in Prussian authority in central Europe led to the Franco-Prussian War in 1870. Faced with a French threat, the southern German states joined Prussia, as Bismarck had planned. The war with France was swiftly concluded in Prussia's favor. In the glow of victory, the new German Empire was created in defeated France at the palace of Versailles. The constitution was ostensibly liberal—it included universal male suffrage and a representative legislative assembly—but the government was responsive only to the chancellor and his professional bureaucracy. Unification led to the establishment of a single national market, a single financial system, and unified national economies that rapidly capitalized industrialization.

E. The United States: Civil War and Reunification

In the United States, the end of the Civil War led to the establishment of a single national market, a single financial system, and unified national economies that rapidly capitalized industrialization.

F. Nationalism and Force

The statesmen of the second half of the nineteenth century created a new sense of what a nation was. Nations achieved mythical form complete with symbolic representation. Nations submerged regional differences and ethnic variation in the unity of the state. In the name of the state, force became an acceptable alternative to diplomacy. Violence and nationalism were simply two aspects of the modern state.

III.   Reforming European Society

   A. Introduction

   In the third quarter of the nineteenth century, the newly centralized states took over the role of social reform. The end result was greater unity of the people around the nation state.

   B. The Second Empire in France, 1852-1870

   The architect of the Second Empire was Louis Napoleon, nephew of the first Napoleon. Elected president of the Second Republic because of his innocuous image and on the basis of promises to all classes of French society, Napoleon III became a dictator in 1851 and emperor in 1852. His reign was typified by economic growth fueled by greater demand for French products and the establishment of a private banking system. The state also invested in a railway system and rebuilt Paris under the direction of Baron Georges Haussmann, prefect of the Seine. The rebuilt center of the city was reserved for the bourgeoisie; the poor were relegated to the suburbs. Louis Napoleon's grandiose foreign policy was less successful. France declared war on Russia in the Crimea and supported the ambitions of Italian nationalists against Austria. While these gained little for France, they did no harm. Napoleon also ordered construction of the Suez Canal and negotiated a free-trade policy with Great Britain. The French intervention in Mexico, however, was an abject diplomatic failure that damaged Napoleon's prestige as a power broker. The military reputation of the French was demolished along with their armies in the Franco-Prussian War. Defeat brought the downfall of the Second Empire and autocratic liberalism.

   C. The Victorian Compromise

   Despite relative political tranquillity, Britain experienced serious social problems. What allowed Britain to avoid revolution was the ability of its representative body, Parliament, to balance industrial growth with protection of the working classes. Between 1832 and 1884, the vote was continually extended to more males, although females remained outside the electorate. Two politicians—the Liberal, William Gladstone, and the Conservative, Benjamin Disraeli—dominated English politics in the latter half of the nineteenth century. Gladstone fostered free trade through the elimination of tariffs, cut military costs, and lowered taxes. He also began the inflammatory policy of removing some of the most onerous symbols of British rule in Ireland by disestablishing the Anglican Church there. Gladstone's Liberal policies also reformed the civil service, introduced the secret ballot, and began a state public education system. Disraeli sponsored more direct state intervention on behalf of the working classes. A new Factory Act limited working hours, the Public Health Act established standards for sanitation, and the Artisans Dwelling Act set regulations for public housing. Under Disraeli's leadership, Parliament even sanctioned legal trade unionism. British political evolution combined free enterprise, a Liberal program, with active state intervention on behalf of the proletariat, a Conservative agenda. The lack of political rigidity within the British electoral system permitted both viewpoints to moderate the impact of industrialization.

D. Reforming Russia

Because of the autocratic nature of the Russian government, all reform had to initiate with the tsar's government. The primary problem was the continued existence of serfdom in Russia. Tsar Alexander II began the process of abolishing serfdom within the agricultural system in response to the perceived need for modernizing the economy to compete with western rivals. In 1861 the tsar emancipated serfs in Russia, granting land to the former peasants in return for payments to be paid over forty-nine years. Land was assigned to peasant communes or *mirs* rather than individuals as a means of ensuring payment. The *mirs* also continued to tie peasants to the land and prevented landless mobility. Although a reform of unprecedented scale, the emancipation of the serfs did not resolve peasant grievances. The tsar was able to enact other reforms of the judiciary and the army and to create local parliamentary bodies, but he failed to quiet criticism of his regime. Reforms did not satisfy the Russian intelligentsia, who continued to protest the order of Russian society. The government attempted to suppress the student-led critics, who turned to radicalization of the peasantry as a means of overthrowing the state. The tsar's government initiated trials that forced many of the intellectuals to flee to the West. A few of the radicals resorted to terrorism in the form of attempted assassination of public officials, including the tsar.

E. The Politics of Leadership

The practice of politics changed in Europe after 1850. Autocratic monarchy existed nowhere outside of Russia. The new source of political leadership were those who could harness the will of the empowered citizens. Molding public opinion became an important aspect of exercising power. One of the means of manipulating public opinion was careful use of the press. The new political leaders tended to view decisions strictly on the basis of the growth of the state, not on grounds of traditional morality. As states were permanently in a state of competition, the new breed of politicians always considered the use of force as a positive good. The final judgment of political success was the success of the nation, not the career of the individual. Political leaders at the end of the nineteenth century risked all to advance the interests of the state.

IV. Changing Values and the Force of New Ideas

A. Introduction

The second half of the nineteenth century witnessed the emergence of materialist values and new ideas that sought to restore order to an industrialized society.

B. The Politics of Homemaking

The domestic household reflected other social changes within European society, although the dichotomy between the bourgeoisie and the working class remained obvious. Home was both a shelter and a demonstration of status. Middle-class women, freed from the industrial workplace, achieved the position of guardian of domesticity. They were responsible for preparation of food and the maintenance of the quality of life within the home. Cleanliness was regarded as emblematic of virtue in the middle-class lifestyle. Working-class women remained in the nineteenth-century workforce and had little time to add to the objects of domestic status or to clean and cook. The working-class family did not share the moral standards of the bourgeoisie. Working women were still regarded as immoral for failing to care for their families. A few women refused to accept society's prescribed roles. The nineteenth century saw the elevation of the cult of domesticity to a standard of middle-class virtue, but also witnessed the beginnings of feminism.

C. Realism in the Arts

Realism rejected the romantic ethos of the arts and the bourgeois definition of morality. Realists attacked the more sordid aspects of industrialized society. Charles Dickens in England portrayed nineteenth-century society as soulless exploitation of the working classes. In France, Flaubert ridiculed the middle-class concepts of morality in *Madame Bovary*. Fyodor Dostoyevsky introduced realism to Russian literature. The development of photography provided a new way to record the reality of the world, people and events.

D. Charles Darwin and the New Science

Charles Darwin, a biologist, offered a new explanation for change in the natural world—evolution through the principle of natural selection. Better adapted species survived to reproduce in greater numbers, thus outstripping less fortunate rivals in their ecological niche. Darwin's theory became immediately controversial and popular. His ideas represented a realist conception of progress based on natural struggle. The "survival of the fittest" replicated the application of force in international relations. Darwin's ideas were also applied to a wide range of theories of social organization.

E. Karl Marx and the Science of Society

Influenced in his early intellectual development by the work of Georg Friedrich Hegel, Marx was exiled from his native Prussia because of his political radicalism. In England he united with Friedrich Engels and developed the concept of dialectical materialism. All societies divided into classes were doomed to destruction as a result of internal conflict between social groups who owned property versus those who did not. Marx argued that labor was the source of all value, but capitalism alienated workers from the fruits of their labor. The constant impoverishment of the proletariat, according to Marx, would lead inevitably to revolution against the economic system. While much of Marx's economic theory was flawed, it provided a focus for working-class political action. In 1864 the

103

International Working Men's Association was formed in London. It was intended to be an international alliance of workers dedicated to the overthrow of capitalism.

F. A New Revolution?

When Napoleon III and his army surrendered to Prussia in 1870, the citizens of Paris continued to resist. From September 1870 until the armistice in January 1871, the Parisians endured starvation and bombardment without capitulating to the German invaders. The rest of France, however, was eager for an end to the conflict. French national elections in 1871 established a new, conservative government dedicated to ending the war. The Parisians felt betrayed. Alienated from the new French government, Parisian citizens refused to disarm. When the government attempted to impose its authority on the city, Paris expelled the national army and founded the Paris Commune. Between March and May 1871, Paris was at war with the remainder of France. In the end, the national armies put an end to the social experiment, but the Paris Commune remained a symbol for revolutionary movements—including Marxism.

TIMELINE

Insert the following events into the timeline. This should help you to compare important historical events chronologically.

kingdom of Italy proclaimed   publication of *On the Origin of Species*
end of Crimean War   assassination of Alexander II of Russia
German empire proclaimed   Seven Weeks' War between Prussia and
                                                 Austria

1856	
1859	
1861	
1866	
1871	
1881	

TERMS, PEOPLE, EVENTS

The following terms, people, and events are important to your understanding of the chapter. Define each one.

Crimean War   Peace of Paris of 1856   *Risorgimento*
Camillo Benso di Cavour   Victor Emmanuel II   Giuseppe Garibaldi
Red Shirts   Otto von Bismarck   *realpolitik*
Seven Weeks' War   Franco-Prussian War   Archduke Maximilian
Napoleon III   Second Empire   Benito Juarez
Paris Commune   Reform Bill of 1832   William E. Gladstone
Benjamin Disraeli   Alexander II   Charles Darwin
natural selection   Social Darwinism   evolution
Karl Marx   *Das Kapital*   labor theory of value
Eastern Question   Realism   Reichstag
Resorgimento   *Zemstvos*   Proclamation of the German
                                                               Empire

MAP EXERCISE

The following exercise is intended to clarify the geophysical environment and the spatial relationships among the important objects and places mentioned in the chapter.

1. How did the establishment of Italy and Germany change the traditional balance of European politics? Compare this map with the map exercise from Chapter 22. How was the Europe of 1870 fundamentally different from the Europe of 1850?

2. Locate the following places on the map.

    boundary of the Kingdom of Italy
    boundary of the German Empire

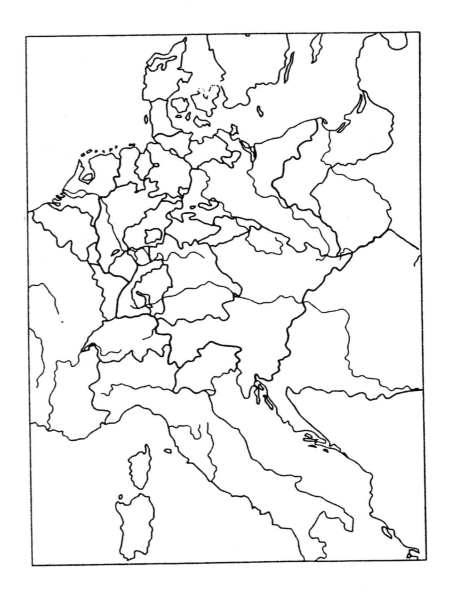

MAKING CONNECTIONS

The following questions are intended to emphasize important ideas within the chapter.

1. Compare and contrast the unifications of Germany and Italy. Consider the leaders of unification, the methods used, the role of warfare, and the role of France.

2. What were the three models for nineteenth-century reform? How did the reforms work in each of the countries considered? Where was reform most successful?

3. In what ways were Darwinism and Marxism similar? How were they symptomatic of the later nineteenth century?

PUTTING LARGER CONCEPTS TOGETHER

The following questions test your ability to summarize the major conclusions of the chapter.

1. How was post-1850 Europe different from the Europe of the Congress of Vienna? What accounts for the differences?

2. How would you respond to the following thesis? "Political relations in Europe after 1850 were predicated on the principles of conflict rather than stability." How did the scientific and economic theories developed during this period reflect this shift?

SELF-TEST OF FACTUAL INFORMATION

1. Which of the following politicians does NOT belong in the group of post-1848 state builders?

    a. Louis Napoleon
    b. Camillo Benso di Cavour
    c. Klemens von Metternich
    d. Otto von Bismarck

2. Bismarck launched wars against all the following nations EXCEPT

    a. Austria.
    b. Denmark.
    c. France.
    d. Russia.

3. After Napoleon III's surrender in 1870,

    a. Rome accepted German rule.
    b. a separate government was established in the southern city of Vichy.
    c. his son succeeded him as Louis Philippe.
    d. Paris fought on and eventually formed a commune.

4. Which of the following was NOT a reform passed during the ministry of William E. Gladstone?

    a. passage of the Trade Union Act
    b. abolition of tariffs
    c. disestablishing the Anglican Church in Ireland
    d. introduction of the secret ballot

5. The most important reform of the reign of Tsar Alexander II was the

    a. creation of a democratic national legislature.
    b. abolition of serfdom.
    c. passage of a public health act.
    d. Limitation of hours worked by children in Russian factories.

6. The theory propounded by Charles Darwin to account for the development of the natural world was

    a. relativity.
    b. heliocentrism.
    c. evolution.
    d. positivism.

7. The labor theory of value was developed by

    a. Emmeline Pankburst.
    b. Karl Marx.
    c. Niels Bohr.
    d. Alfred Marshall.

8. What was the school that attempted to apply the theory of evolution to gender and racial distinctions?

    a. Social Realism
    b. Labor theory of value
    c. Kipling conceptualism
    d. Social Darwinism

9. What organization did Marxists help to found in London in 1864?

    a. the BUF
    b. the International Working Men's Association
    c. the Charter Society
    d. the Fabian Society

10. Who was Karl Marx's collaborator and patron in England?

    a. Alexander Pushkin
    b. Friedrich Engels
    c. Charles Darwin
    d. Arthur Balfour

CHAPTER 24

The Crisis of European Culture, 1871–1914

OUTLINE

I.   Speeding to the Future

The futurist movement wanted to break all ties with the past and to disregard the heritage of Western civilization. Futurists at the end of the nineteenth century perceived a moral and cultural crisis and proposed a radical solution. Traditional values seemed to have no place in an increasingly industrialized world. Change, technology, the masses, and violence were the watchwords of the new culture.

II.   European Economy and the Politics of Mass Society

    A. Introduction

Industrialization and urbanization typified the economy of Europe between 1870 and 1914.

    B. Regulating Boom and Bust

Industrial production led to a greater concentration of population in the cities. Those people that remained in the rural areas became increasingly linked to urban and national culture through the new communications and transportation networks. Between 1873 and 1895 the European economy suffered from economic depression. The so-called Great Depression of the nineteenth century was followed by a boom period to 1914. Such radical swings in economic fortunes convinced governments, bankers and industrialists of the necessity of regulating business cycles of boom and bust. Industries of the later nineteenth century had to be heavily capitalized to make use of the new sources of energy—petroleum and electricity. Capital formation to support the new industries had to be obtained from financial institutions, not private family funds. Bankers were unwilling to risk the enormous investments in industrialization unless some of the worst aspects of the business cycle were controlled. Businesses responded by forming cartels and trusts to control the market. Cartels were groups of firms that cooperated to fix prices. Although Great Britain failed to develop cartels, corporations in Germany, Austria, and France organized to control the marketplace. Banks similarly formed groups to fix interest rates. These cooperative financial organizations were called *consortia*. The control of the marketplace sounded the death knell for free trade. European nations returned to tariff barriers to protect domestic industries. Only Britain remained aloof from the policy of protectionism. Tariffs divided Europe into two halves: an industrialized north and west, and an agricultural south and east.

C. Challenging Liberal England

Parliamentary politics saved Britain from revolution. In addition, Britain was less affected by the boom and bust cycle of the late nineteenth century. At the outset of the twentieth century, however, wages stagnated while prices continued to rise. Workers responded by depending more heavily on trade unionism for political influence. A new leader—Keir Hardie, a miner—launched a political experiment, the Labour party. Hardie attempted to get trade unions to support working class candidates for Parliament in preference to the traditional political elites of the Conservative or Liberal parties. Intellectuals also assaulted the traditional British political system. Fabian socialists called for gradual change. Under the leadership of the Webbs, G. B. Shaw, and others, the Fabians supported the new Labour party. In response to the working-class threat, the Liberals introduced legislative reform for laborers. Unions were permitted to engage in more aggressive strike tactics and a national health system was introduced. Most radical of the reforms was the Parliament Bill of 1911 that lopped off most of the constitutional powers of the House of Lords, the most conservative branch of Parliament. Reform did not stifle protest. Unions increased in number, as did the frequency of job actions against sensitive industries such railroads, coal mining, and dock workers. In addition, women increasingly pressed for the right to vote. At the same time parliament remained unable to resolve the issue of Irish home rule.

D. Political Struggles in Germany

German males could vote, but the Reichstag had limited powers in the German constitution. In general, Bismarck was able to cooperate with political liberals to build German industry and commercial infrastructure. He also launched an attack, the Kulturkampf, on Roman Catholics who were suspected of undermining loyalty to the state. Bismarck also targeted socialists as potential political enemies. The chancellor outlawed the Social Democratic party, a German Marxist group. Despite repression, both Catholics and Socialists continued to field candidates. When Bismarck was dismissed in a conflict with Wilhelm II, the Social Democrats became the largest political party in the Reichstag. German Marxism practiced revisionism, the political position that capitalism would wither away without violent revolution. The foremost politician of the Social Democrats was Eduard Bernstein, who sought to gain an alliance with the German labor movement. Unions were recruited to the Social Democrat cause. In fear of the growing power of the socialist and trade union movement, conservatives attempted to consolidate support among agricultural and capitalist industrial groups. Aggressive foreign policy and super-patriotism were the hallmarks of right-wing politics in Germany.

E. Political Scandals and Mass Politics in France

The Third Republic was the offspring of surrender in the Franco-Prussian War and the bloody suppression of the Paris Commune. Despite its rough beginnings, the Third Republic was able to marshal public support through the creation of a national public education system that broke down regionalism within the country. Communication networks and control of the press helped to create a national mass culture. The French right wing was attracted to General Georges Boulanger who presented himself as a national "super-patriot" and war hero. Some conservatives saw him as the candidate best suited to restore the monarchy. By 1889 Boulanger had built a sufficient support base to threaten the Third Republic. In the end, the general fled the country under a cloud of treason, but he had galvanized a right-wing movement poised to take advantage of national patriotism. The Dreyfus affair also stirred political emotions in France. Dreyfus, a Jew, was an army officer accused of selling state secrets to the Germans. Dreyfus' conviction on charges of treason was largely due to anti-Semitism and xenophobia. Right-wing political groups supported the conviction, but those on the left of the political spectrum pointed to perjuries and extraordinary decisions that invalidated the trial. Dreyfus was exonerated and pardoned in 1905, but the dispute over his prosecution created new political alliances on both sides of the question. Pressure groups utilized the press to bring pressure on the government.

F. Defeating Liberalism in Austria

The Dual Monarchy of Austria-Hungary was a constitutional monarchy politically dominated by the capitalist middle class. The symbol of bourgeois affectation was the rebuilding of the Austrian capital of Vienna after 1860. In reality, the power of the bourgeoisie was limited. As a class, the Austrian bourgeoisie was smaller than those of western Europe and too dependent on its partnership with the Habsburg emperors. By 1900 the liberalism of the Austrian middle class was supplanted by more conservative groups. The right wing was able to capitalize on general dissatisfaction with the capitalist political leadership. Mass political organizations emerged around Pan-Germanism, anti-Semitism, anticapitalism of the rural classes, and superpatriotism. In the election for mayor of Vienna in 1895, Jews were identified with capitalism as a means of sweeping liberals out of office. With them went faith in the parliamentary forms of government.

III. Outsiders in Mass Politics

A. Introduction

Mass politics were the order of the day at the end of the nineteenth century. A few groups—women, Jews, and ethnic minorities—were left outside the new political alliances. Some few others—the anarchists—rejected participation in the normal political processes.

B. Feminists and Politics

Women remained grossly underpaid in comparison to male laborers. They were excluded from political participation, subject to the domination of husbands in marriage, and excluded from public education. Feminists at the end of the nineteenth century began to form mass political organizations. The first international meeting of feminists met in Paris in 1878. Most women, however, continued to accept passively the roles prescribed for them in the cult of domesticity. National feminist groups varied in their political objectives: those who wanted the right to vote and those who wanted economic, social and legal reforms to gain equality with men in society. Socialist women were primarily among the latter group. In order to achieve their ends, feminists formed political action groups. Of the feminist organizations, the British suffrage movement was most effective. Led by Emmeline Pankhurst, the Women's Social and Political Union successfully created a public forum for women's issues. In 1910, following a parliamentary failure to pass voting rights for women, a battle between suffragists and the police turned bloody. Black Friday stimulated a more militant attitude on the part of English feminists. Suffragettes turned to vandalism and violence as political statements. The government responded by more repressive tactics of imprisonment. The movement accomplished little before 1914, but English women were granted limited political rights in 1918. Women's movements had little more success outside Britain. German women could vote after 1918, American women in 1920, and French women only in 1945. The groups more intent on social reform than the franchise separated from the suffragettes. Women's socialist movements were most numerous in Germany. Women socialists often faced opposition from male socialists who remained threatened by women in the workforce.

C. The Jewish Question and Zionism

Anti-Semitism, the hatred of Jews, was common in the nineteenth century. Most severe persecution occurred in Russia following the assassination of Alexander II. Jews from eastern Europe began a slow migration westward to Germany and to the United States. Within nations, Jews moved from the countryside to cities. Even where the new Jewish communities achieved political rights, they remained targets of bigotry as threats to local economic and commercial elites. Fear of the Jews culminated in the anti-liberal politics of Germany and Austria at the turn of the century. Some Jewish leaders responded to anti-Semitism by proposing a separate nation for Jews—a political solution called Zionism first suggested by Theodor Herzl. The appeal of Zionism was particularly strong in eastern Europe. Jews began migrating to Palestine, the ancient homeland of the Israelites, in the first decades of the twentieth century. Even some Jewish leaders recognized the potential difficulties inherent in migration to Arab Palestine, but the movement continued despite the potential for violence.

D. Workers and Minorities on the Margins

Anarchism was the total rejection of the political system. Some anarchists turned to terrorism: attacks on private property and assassination. Anarchists were just as negative toward the new mass political organizations as they were to liberal institutions. Anarchism made heaviest philosophical inroads in Russia. Mikhail Bakunin became the leading anarchist theorist (if such a theory could be said to have existed). He was followed as the leading proponent of anarchism by Prince Petr Kropotkin. Anarchism was more popular as a form of political action in less industrialized countries of western Europe. In France anarchism allied with trade unionism in a movement called *syndicalism.* As a result, trade unionism remained outside the parliamentary political structure. The spokesman of anarcho-syndicalism was Georges Sorel.

IV.   Shaping the New Consciousness

A. Introduction

Science and technology began to reshape the known world between 1870 and 1914. Science challenged traditional belief systems in the most fundamental fashion.

B. The Authority of Science

The late nineteenth century was an age of scientific discovery. In the physical sciences electromagnetism, X-rays, visible light, and radio waves all were discovered. Additions were made to the table of chemical elements. Max Planck proposed quantum physics to replace classical theory. Einstein expanded Planck's discoveries to include a theory of relativity that assaulted Newtonian theories of gravity. Biological sciences experienced similar iconoclasm. Biological research centered on the identification of microorganisms associated with disease. One by one epidemic diseases were brought under control. Such knowledge was disseminated through public health services, resulting in improvements in sanitation and disease prevention. Scientists became the discoverers and creators of a new world of knowledge.

C. Establishing the Social Sciences

Scientific methodology was also applied to social organization with similarly traumatic results. History, archaeology, and economics were subjected to scientific techniques. Psychology became divided between behavioralists like Ivan Pavlov, who studied behavioral reactions to external stimuli, and psychoanalysts like Sigmund Freud, who probed the landscape of the unconscious. Science could also be utilized to create new social theories. Criminologists attempted to identify criminal "types" through physical appearance. The social climate became, itself, the object of study. Emile Durkheim was the first modern sociologist to argue that deviation was the result of environmental factors. Geneticists argued that heredity determined biologically the causes of social variation. At the same time scientific ideas were used to attack traditions. Moral values and religion.

D. The "New Woman" and the New Consciousness

Social science was utilized to demonstrate the inferiority of women. Darwin's theories of eternal struggle were buttressed with biological studies that "proved" the physical impossibility of women competing with men on an equal footing. Women, according to the scientific studies, were best suited to their domestic tasks and reproduction. In response to scientific subjection, the "new woman" emerged. The new woman wanted to smash the feminine image created by the cult of domesticity and male domination. In the pursuit of independence, the new woman sought full social equality with males. Included in that concept of equality was control of the process of reproduction. Public dissemination of birth control devices and knowledge of reproduction and sexuality was a goal of the new woman.

E. Art and the New Age

Late-nineteenth century art influenced by the new ideas, scientific discoveries and values gave rise to new artistic forms and movements that reflected the new middle class. Impressionism chose unlikely subjects for their paintings, while symbolists were concerned with the unconscious.

F. The New Consumption

By the end of the nineteenth century, the benefits of industrialization had spread to the working class. As the money economy reached more layers of European society, the consumption of goods became a measure of social status. Department stores pandering to the demands for consumer goods first emerged in the late 1800s. Leisure was available for sale—in resorts for the middle class, in pubs and taverns for the working class. The poorer members of society were also attracted to inexpensive strip shows and cinemas. Organized sports became popular forms of mass culture.

TIMELINE

Insert the following events into the timeline. This should help you to compare important historical events chronologically.

Keir Hardie elected to British Commons
beginning of Kulturkampf
beginning of Dreyfus trial

Einstein's theory of relativity
nineteenth century Great Depression begins
formation of Women's Social and Political
   Union

1872	
1873	
1892	
1894	
1903	
1905	

TERMS, PEOPLE, EVENTS

The following terms, people, and events are important to your understanding of the chapter. Define each one.

Futurists
Margaret Sanger
Anarchism
Marie Curie
Alfred Marshall
Feminists
anti-Semitism
Consortium
Pogroms
Women's Social and Political
   Union

David Lloyd George
Sigmund Freud
Mikhail Bakunin
Albert Einstein
Emile Durkheim
Emmeline Pankhurst
Zionism
James Keir Hardie
revisionism
Eugenics

Kulturkampf
Thorstein Veblen
James Clerk Maxwell
Dreyfus affair
Boular ger affair
Theodor Herzl
cartels
Labour party
Impressionism
Fabians

MAKING CONNECTIONS

The following questions are intended to emphasize important ideas within the chapter.

1. What was mass politics? In what ways did mass politics affect Britain, Germany, Austria, and France?

2. What was feminism? What gains were made during the nineteenth century?

3. Define Zionism? How did it advance during the nineteenth century?

4. What were the advances in the natural sciences? What were the advances in the social sciences?

5. How were both based on "scientific models" of study and research?

PUTTING LARGER CONCEPTS TOGETHER

The following questions test your ability to summarize the major conclusions of the chapter.

1. Was the attempt to incorporate mass politics into the European consciousness essentially democratic? If not, what did it reflect?

2. In what way could it be said that the "new consciousness" of the later nineteenth century reflected changes in European society brought about by industrialization? How did this "new consciousness" compare to the Enlightenment?

SELF-TEST OF FACTUAL INFORMATION

1. The French impressionist painters

   a. were similar to the futurists in that they embraced the new age.
   b. differed from the futurists in that they were optimistic.
   c. differed from the futurists in that they were pessimistic.
   d. broke with the traditional forms by emphasizing the private lives of the bourgeoisie.

2. During the period 1871-1914, Europe witnessed a tremendous growth in

   a. agricultural development and the rise of agricultural capitalism.
   b. Asian intrusion into European domestic affairs.
   c. the flight of the urban poor back to the countryside.
   d. heavy industry and the increasing urbanization of European populations.

3. The only major power to retain a policy of free trade in the late nineteenth century was

   a. Russia.
   b. Spain.
   c. France.
   d. Great Britain.

4. For what group did James Keir Hardie attract national attention in Britain during the late nineteenth century?

   a. the BUF
   b. the Chartists
   c. the Labour Party
   d. the Liberal Party

5. By what year had the German Social Democratic Party become the largest single party in Germany?

   a. 1914
   b. 1870
   c. 1848
   d. 1825

6. The Boulanger and Dreyfus affairs illustrate

   a. the danger of militarism.
   b. the greater efficiency of democracy in France.
   c. the major role of the press in formulating public opinion.
   d. the innate tendency of the French government toward absolutism.

7. The rejection of liberalism in late nineteenth- and early twentieth-century Austria could be tied to all the following factors except

   a. nationalist aspirations of the lower middle class.
   b. anti-Semitism.
   c. growing fears of government-sponsored discrimination.
   d. rejection of bourgeois domination of parliamentary politics.

8. The founder of Zionism in its political form was

   a. Theodor Herzl.
   b. Georg von Schonerer.
   c. Clara Zetkin.
   d. Theodor Mommsen.

9. Max Planck, Albert Einstein, and Niels Bohr all made major contributions in the area of

   a. modern physics based on relativity and uncertainty.
   b. classical physics predicated on Newtonian principles.
   c. the role of radioactivity.
   d. electromagnetic theory.

10. Charles Darwin's the *Descent of Man* portrayed women as

    a. possessing less mental power than men.
    b. actually the first Homo sapiens.
    c. superior culturally and scientifically to men.
    d. increasingly independent and self-assured.

CHAPTER 25

Europe and the World, 1870-1914

OUTLINE

I. The Politics of Mapmaking

As European imperialists spread their influence throughout the globe, they wrangled over the issue of mapping their conquests. Most agreed on the necessity of standardization: all nations should measure time and space similarly to prevent confusion. The British, the most successful imperialists, were able to have the Greenwich Observatory outside of London recognized as the place through which the prime meridian ran. The location of the prime meridian was important, because it allowed standardized times to be calculated by longitude. Maps of the world served to depict graphically the success of European imposition of Western influence.

II. The European Balance of Power, 1870-1914

A. Introduction

Rising nationalism at home and imperial tensions abroad were mirrored by deterioration of the European balance of power within the continent.

B. Upsetting the European Balance of Power

The alliance system of Europe was dramatically altered after 1870 with the creation of a united Germany and Italy. Initially, Bismarck allied Germany with Russia and Austria-Hungary in the Three Emperors' League in order to isolate France on the continent. Despite its successful industrialization, Germany was confronted by two geographical limitations: the possibility of its North Sea ports being effectively shut off from the North Atlantic and the absence of any easy frontier for expansion. Austria-Hungary lacked internal unity. Various ethnic groups within the aged empire demanded greater independence. Moreover, the Habsburg had not responded to the challenge of European industrialization and imperialism. Technically outside the European alliance system lay the Ottoman Empire. Weakened over centuries, the Ottoman Empire continued to control a large portion of the Balkan peninsula. Like Austria, the Ottoman Empire was convulsed by movements of various ethnic groups seeking independence. Although western European powers had seized parts of the Ottoman Empire during their imperial expansion, none was willing to accept the demise of the Ottomans if it meant the domination of another European power. The point at which European ambitions and ethnic revolution met was the Balkan peninsula.

C. The Instability of the Alliance System

The new alliance system was predicated on French fear of German aggression and the continued Russian search for access to the Mediterranean. Russia was hopeful of gaining an advantage in southern Europe by fostering Slavic nationalist movements in the Balkan territories of the Ottoman Empire. Supporting a Serbian revolt in two Ottoman principalities with Slavic majorities, Russia declared war on the Ottoman Empire in 1876. Bismarck engineered the peace settlement in the Congress of Berlin in 1878. Russian gains were nullified in the treaty, leading to diplomatic stress between Germany and Russia. German support for Austria-Hungary at the Congress of Berlin resulted in the Dual Alliance of 1879. In 1882 Italy joined Germany and Austria-Hungary to form the Triple Alliance. A second Balkan crisis in 1885 led to diplomatic realignment. Again Germany supported Austria-Hungary's interests at the expense of Russian ambitions in the Balkans. Bismarck maintained the alliance with Russia only with extreme difficulty. After Bismarck's dismissal in 1890, the fragile relationship between Russia and Germany dissolved. Seeking allies, Russia concluded an alliance with France. France also managed an agreement with its former imperial rival, Great Britain. The three—Russia, France, and Great Britain—formed the Triple Entente. Thus the Triple Alliance and the Triple Entente divided Europe into two competing diplomatic spheres. Continued problems within the Balkan peninsula threatened to topple the precarious diplomatic house of cards. Russian and Austrian conflicts over domination of Slavic national movements within the region continued to foment revolutions. Austrian annexation of former Ottoman principalities coveted by Serbia nearly led to war in 1908. Hostilities broke out again in 1913, this time between Serbia (supported by Russia) and Bulgaria (supported by Austria-Hungary). In each case, the alliance system threatened to involve all Europe in acts of violence limited to the Balkan peninsula.

III.   The New Imperialism

A. Introduction

Imperialism was not a creation of the nineteenth century, but industrialization led to the dominance of the more industrialized European nations over the underdeveloped regions of Asia, Africa, and the New World.

B. The Technology of Empire

Technological advances paved the way for European dominance of the world. The advent of steamships shortened the amount of time spent in sea travel and brought all ports of the world closer to Europe in terms of time spent on the seas. Steamships also enabled Europeans to penetrate Africa and Asia on the navigable rivers. Technology permitted the construction of deepwater ports throughout the world. Even more impressively, two canals—the Suez in Egypt and the Panama—provided shortcuts between major oceans. The French began both canals, but as a result of financial mismanagement lost their controlling interests to the British and the Americans. The telegraph shortened the time needed to communicate between European nations and their colonies, thus fostering more efficient military and diplomatic control. New medical discoveries lessened the severity of tropical diseases on European populations. Finally, new types of firearms gave the European military extraordinary advantages over the soldiers of the rest of the world.

C. Motives for Empire

There were many reasons why European nations sought to establish colonies. Not all nations profited from colonial ventures. In general, the major powers—Britain, France, and Germany—controlled the business of empire. In some cases, economic motivation was more a matter of private or corporate initiative rather than national interest. In any case, an international economy was created. Geopolitical interests also affected the pace of imperial expansion. Countries determined that some regions were valuable, not because they had intrinsic economic value, but because they were sensitive regions. For example, the British defended Egypt because of the Suez Canal, the most expedient route to British colonies in the Indian subcontinent. Areas also had to be acquired and defended in order to establish fueling bases for the steamships that carried goods and men around the world. Defense of sensitive regions led to greater expenditures for the establishment of national military forces on both the land and the sea. Military leaders became increasingly important in the determination of foreign policy. Colonies were often pursued to enhance national prestige. Governments competed with one another in a colonial race. Political leaders utilized the issue of colonialism to whip up support for the party or government. Newspapers forged a national public opinion to promote the colonial race or to deflect public attention from problems on the home front. "Jingoism" emerged as a term to describe manipulated patriotism.

IV. The Search for Territory and Markets

A. Introduction

In Africa, where European prejudices dictated that social organization was primitive, even in those areas where large states existed, military conquest and direct political administration was imposed. In Asia, Europeans were more likely to accept existing social hierarchies. Europeans imposed either informal empires, as in China, or formal but indirect rule, as in India.

B. The Scramble for Africa: Diplomacy and Conflict

The European seizure of colonies in Africa extended from 1875 to 1912. There were many rationales for the seizure of colonies: carving out military reputations, mineral wealth, deterioration in traditional trade zones, missionary activity, and the dictates of European strategy. Underlying all the motives was the European conviction that Africans were racially inferior. The process of colonization was viewed as the scientific proof of the racial superiority of whites. A second factor was the downturn in the European economy after 1873 and the subsequent rise of protectionism and economic competition. The person who initiated the scramble for land in Africa was Leopold II, king of Belgium, who seized the area around the Congo River basin for himself. When other

European nations, envious of the economic potential, refused to recognize Leopold's seizure, a conference was convened in Berlin in 1884. The conference at Berlin provided the ground rules for the scramble for Africa—states claiming territory would have to produce proof of economic development in the region claimed. In general, the European seizure of Africa proceeded without warfare among the colonists. The process of claiming colonies, however, was characterized by violence against Africans. Technological advantages such as the machine gun led to the widespread slaughter of indigenous peoples. Despite the overwhelming military advantages enjoyed by Europeans, some African states, such as Ethiopia, resisted colonization. Surrounded by French, British, and Italian colonies, the Ethiopian emperor Menelik II attempted to play off all the European states against one another. He offered territorial concessions to each in return for modern weapons. In 1896 Italy launched an invasion of Ethiopia. Outnumbered and facing an African army equipped with modern arms, the Italians were defeated and forced to recognize Ethiopia as a sovereign state. Ethiopia was the only African state to successfully defend itself against European colonizers.

C. Gold, Empire-Building, and the Boer War

In South Africa the British engaged in a long war with white Africans, the Boers, to control the mineral resources of the region. The British, confident in the isolation of the Boers, had recognized the Afrikaner states of the Transvaal and the Orange Free State after the Great Trek of 1835. German entry into the scramble for imperial possessions awakened British fears of an alliance between the Germans and the Boers. The discovery of gold in the Transvaal in 1886 heightened British concerns. British investors, including Cecil Rhodes, immediately began to capitalize the mining operations of the Transvaal. In 1895 Rhodes attempted to overthrow the Afrikaner government of the Transvaal through the so-called Jameson Raid, which failed. Following the failure of Rhodes' scheme, the British sent a new minister, Alfred Milner, to South Africa. Milner agitated until war between Britain and the Boer republics was inevitable. Warfare broke out in 1899 and lasted until 1902. Both sides suffered horrendous casualties in the fighting. The British annexed the two Boer republics, but agreed not to make any decisions concerning the black African population of South Africa before returning political power to the Afrikaners.

D. Imperialism in Asia

India was the crown jewel of Britain's empire. To protect lines of communication and to establish markets for Indian products, the British government engaged in other colonial ventures throughout the world. One of the trade links was the triangular trade in Indian cottons for Chinese tea that was exported to England. When Chinese demand for Indian cottons waned, the British substituted opium produced in the Indian sub-continent. By the 1830s, opium was one of Britain's most profitable crops. The Chinese government attempted to halt the traffic in narcotics, but the British defended their right to export opium in the Opium War. Between 1842 and 1895, the European powers defeated Chinese attempts to expel foreigners on five occasions. Britain, Germany, Japan, and France carved out "spheres of influence" including ports in China. From the ports, foreign investors linked the coast with the interior by railways. Foreign capitalists gained control of the Chinese economy. Foreign domination of spheres of influence was reflected in the imposition of Western laws and Western administration through consuls. While China barely retained its national identity, other areas of Asia were not so fortunate. The French established control of Indochina; and the British carved out colonies in Burma, Hong Kong and Kowloon. Japan was a late, but determined, entrant into the colonial wars. Japanese armies seized the island of Taiwan from China in 1895 and claimed areas in Manchuria and Korea. Both of the latter claims brought Japan into conflict with Russia. The Japanese enforced their claims in the Russo-Japanese War, 1904-1905, a shocking victory over a weak European opponent.

E. The Imperialism of the United States

American imperialism began with the expansion of the United States across North America. In the process, the United States decimated Native Americans. Rich in natural resources, the United States began rapid industrialization in the nineteenth century. To develop new markets, the U.S. looked to the Pacific and to the Caribbean. Hawaii and Samoa provided fueling stops for American steamships in the Pacific, while repeated intervention in the countries of Latin America resulted in U.S. hegemony in the Caribbean.

V   Results of a European Dominated World

A. Introduction

The Europeans intended to shape the new colonial empires in their own images' but the creation of empire imposed social and cultural changes on Europe, as well.

B. A World Economy

Colonization created a worldwide international market with Europe as its industrialized center. In the process, traditional economies of colonies were altered or destroyed to produce commodities valued in Europe. Investment capital flowed out of the industrialized West into eastern Europe and the colonies in search of more rapid returns on investments. Britain remained the greatest commercial giant, but Germany and the United States had begun to challenge her dominance by the twentieth century. Capital investment and trade was related to the growing demand for state protection of commercial interests.

C. Race and Culture

Europeans approached colonial peoples from a position of racial superiority. Racism received its pseudo-scientific basis from evolutionary theories gaining currency in the second half of the nineteenth century. Europeans regarded themselves as the cultural and racial overlords of the rightfully subjugated peoples of the colonies.

D. Women and Imperialism

In the age of imperialism, European women were encouraged to have more children to ensure the survival of the superior white race. Careful breeding, based on the "science" of eugenics, was intended to improve offspring. The burden of racial improvement fell on women. Women who served in the colonies were expected to preserve the dignity and status of Western culture.

E. Ecology and Imperialism

The process of imperialism disrupted native ecologies. While there were some improvements in medical care and some modern technology was introduced, in general the impact of Western civilization was negative. Tribal societies simply disintegrated, to be replaced by corrupt and inadequate hierarchies dependent on colonial intervention for survival. Asian and African laborers, once converted to production for Western markets, became dependent on business cycles within those markets. Labor instability contributed to breakdown of tribal organization, as workers migrated from one place to another in search of employment. The most extreme case of ecological disregard of colonial territories was the exportation of criminals to prison colonies.

F. Critiquing Capitalism

Not everyone saw the imperial race as a positive good. Some condemned it as exploitative and racist. In *Imperialism, A Study*, J. A. Hobson criticized imperialism as a poor solution to the problems of industrialization. Nikolai Lenin, a Russian socialist, argued that imperialism marked the last, decadent stage of capitalism. While both works were flawed, they marked the beginning of debate over the morality and economic realities of imperialism. Most Europeans, as judged by electoral results and the press, clearly endorsed imperial policies. The sense of the superiority of European culture and of the white race remained dominant.

TIMELINE

Insert the following events into the timeline. This should help you to compare important historical events chronologically.

Italy invades Ethiopia
Leopold claims Congo River basin
Opium War begins

end of the Boer War
formal British rule in India begins
Berlin Conference establishes ground rules for
    colonialism

1839	
1861	
1876	
1885	
1896	
1902	

TERMS, PEOPLE, EVENTS

The following terms, people, and events are important to your understanding of the chapter. Define each one.

prime meridian
Ferdinand de Lesseps
scramble for Africa
Congo Free State
Menelik II
Alfred Milner
spheres of influence
Sino-Japanese War
J. A. Hobson
Balkan peninsula
Quinine
International African
    Association

new imperialism
geopolitics
Leopold II
Berlin Conference of 1884
Cecil Rhodes
Boer War
treaty ports
Russo-Japanese War
Vladimir Ilich Ulyanov
Berlin Congress of 1878
Extraterritoriality
Balkan crises

Suez Canal
Jingoism
Triple Alliance
machine gun
Jameson Raid
Opium War
extraterritoriality
white man's burden
Three Emperors' League
Triple Entente
Battle of Adowa

MAP EXERCISE

The following exercise is intended to clarify the geophysical environment and the spatial relationships among the important objects and places mentioned in the chapter.

1. Compare the colonial holdings of the European nations in 1914 to the colonial ventures of the seventeenth century. What nations became more significant as imperial powers? What nations ceased to play a major role in worldwide imperialism? How does this reflect the political changes in Europe?

2. Locate the following places on the map.

Ethiopia	Suez Canal	Japan
Ottoman Empire	The Balkans	Belgium
France	Portugal	England
China		

3. Mark the colonial possessions of the following countries:

    Great Britain, France, Germany, Portugal, and Belgium.

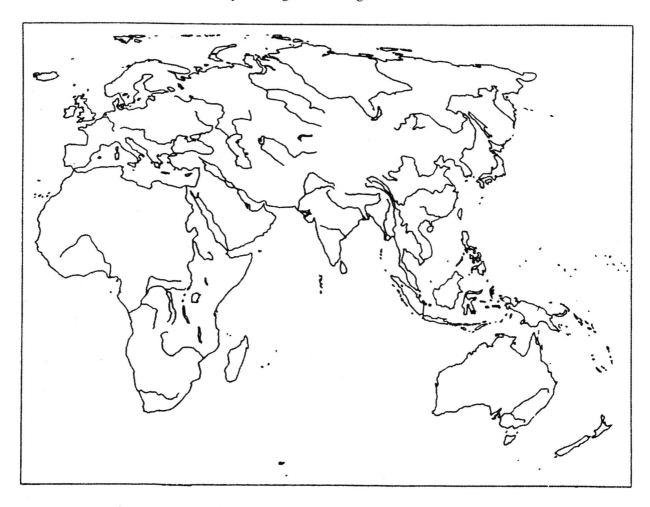

MAKING CONNECTIONS

The following questions are intended to emphasize important ideas within the chapter.

1. Define "new imperialism." What technology made European imperialism possible? What were the motives for imperialism?

2. How did the "scramble for Africa" begin? How did European nations relate to each other during the scramble? How did they react to indigenous peoples?

3. What was the cause of the Boer War? What was its outcome?

4. What forms of imperialism were imposed on India and China? Which could be considered formal rule, which informal? What non-European nation was involved in Asian imperialism?

5. What were the results of a European-dominated world?

6. What were the liberal and socialist critiques of imperialism?

7. What were the geopolitical realities of Europe at the end of the nineteenth century? What alliances were the result? What destabilized the alliance system?

PUTTING LARGER CONCEPTS TOGETHER

The following questions test your ability to summarize the major conclusions of the chapter.

1. What was "new imperialism?" How did it differ from the imperial and colonial systems of the fifteenth through seventeenth centuries? How did the impact of "new imperialism" differ from that of the earlier variety?

2. In what way was the "new imperialism" an outgrowth of the Industrial Revolution and of the altered political configuration of Europe after 1850?

SELF-TEST OF FACTUAL INFORMATION

1. Which of the following statements about "new imperialism" is NOT accurate?

    a. Nations acquired territories on an intense and unprecedented scale.
    b. Industrial powers dominated the nonindustrial world.
    c. None of the European nations that had held colonies prior to 1870 participated.
    d. Only nation-states commanded the technology and resources necessary for the new scale of imperialist expansion.

2. What nation was responsible for the construction of the Suez Canal, completed in 1869?

    a. Britain
    b. France
    c. Germany
    d. Russia

3. Which of the following statements concerning the motivations for imperialism is NOT accurate?

    a. Almost all colonies were economically valuable.
    b. Some colonies were important due to proximity to other colonies, important sea lanes, or as fueling stations.
    c. European statesmen used imperialism as a means of enhancing national prestige.
    d. Western newspapers deliberately fostered the desire for the advancement of national interests.

4. What person provided the catalyst for the "scramble for Africa"?

    a. Alfred Milner
    b. Queen Victoria
    c. Leopold II of Belgium
    d. Otto von Bismarck of Germany

5. What African nation most successfully resisted European imperialism at the end of the nineteenth century?

    a. Ethiopia
    b. Zimbabwe
    c. Libya
    d. South Africa

6. All of the following contributed to the outbreak of the Boer War EXCEPT

   a. the emancipation of all black slaves in the Transvaal and Orange Free State.
   b. the fear of German intervention in the Boer republics.
   c. the discovery of large gold deposits.
   d. the Jameson Raid.

7. What was the most important of the British colonial possessions and the starting point for all British expansion?

   a. South Africa
   b. India
   c. Egypt
   d. Singapore

8. Which of the following statements concerning European imperialism in China is NOT accurate?

   a. The first European conflict with China was over the protection of the European opium trade.
   b. By 1912 over fifty Chinese ports had been handed over to Europeans as treaty ports.
   c. Europeans rapidly established formal empires within China.
   d. The construction of railroads opened up new areas of China to European claims.

9. Which of the following statements best summarizes J.A. Hobson's critique of European imperialism?

   a. Capitalism is inherently and inevitably imperialistic.
   b. World War I was the final "imperialist war."
   c. Imperialism only failed because the European governments were unable to establish strong governments in their colonies.
   d. Rather than create new opportunities for investment in home markets' European entrepreneurs sought higher profits abroad.

10. Which of the following nations was NOT a member of the Triple Alliance?

    a. Germany
    b. Russia
    c. Italy
    d. Austria-Hungary

CHAPTER 26

War and Revolution, 1914-1920

OUTLINE

I.   Selling the Great War

In order to maintain public support for war efforts, governments turned to advertising techniques to sell the necessity of continuing national sacrifices. The successful prosecution of war required support on the home front—a partnership between the warriors on the lines and the producers of food and weapons at home. In the First World War, the need for personal sacrifice was the dominant theme of government appeals.

II.   The War Europe Expected

     A. Introduction

Industrialized Europe viewed itself as the center of the world—economically, socially, culturally, and militarily. European statesmen recognized the use of power for limited purposes, but could not comprehend the travesty of a global conflict. War, when fought, would be swiftly concluded. The faith in limited warfare made statesmen more willing to engage in diplomatic brinkmanship.

     B. Separating Friends from Foes

In 1914 Europe was divided into two alliance systems. The Triple Entente of Britain, France, and Russia faced the Triple Alliance of Germany, Austria-Hungary, and Italy. Smaller nations were allied with one or another of the blocs. The alliance systems included irrevocable sets of circumstances leading all the participants into war. Weaker nations could act in the full knowledge that their actions had to be supported by more powerful allies.

     C. Military Timetables

Military considerations affected all diplomatic decisions. German war preparations were embodied in the Schlieffen Plan, a grand strategy that committed all German forces to the western front against France rather than splitting German armies to face both France and Russia. General Schlieffen believed that the more primitive Russian transportation system would not allow the eastern enemies to mobilize before France could be defeated. Russia, too, considered the problems of mobilization. The answer of Russian generals was to mobilize along the entire front with Germany and Austria-Hungary before the declaration of war. Thus mobilization led inevitably to war. The French grand strategy, Plan XVII, was designed to attack Germany immediately in case of the outbreak of war. Unfortunately, the plan did not account for a German attack through neutral Belgium. In all cases, the need for speed in mobilization limited diplomatic responses to potential conflict.

D. Assassination at Sarajevo

The inexorable path to war was begun in the Austrian province of Bosnia, recently annexed in the Balkans. A Slavic nationalist, Gavrilo Princip assassinated the designated heir to the Austrian throne, Archduke Franz Ferdinand. Neither the event nor the participants seemed important at the time, but the event involved the sensitive issue of control of the Balkan Peninsula. Russia and Austria-Hungary were permanent rivals for dominance in the region. The assassination served as a pretext for Austria-Hungary to declare war on the independent Slavic state of Serbia, an ally of Russia. As Austria-Hungary launched an invasion, the Russians mobilized along their entire front. Germany declared war in response to Russian mobilization on the eastern front and simultaneously declared war on France as the Schlieffen Plan required. Britain remained temporarily aloof, then joined the other members of the Triple Entente. An imperial incident in the Balkans dragged all the major powers of Europe into war.

III. A New Kind of Warfare

A. Introduction

The war Europe got was not what had been expected. It could neither be limited in scope nor duration. The countries of the Triple Entente joined by Italy and Japan faced the Central Powers of Germany and Austria-Hungary joined by the Ottoman Empire.

B. Technology and the Trenches

Much of nineteenth-century warfare had been predicated on speed and maneuverability, but the First World War on the western front almost immediately was limited to the trenches that ran from the English Channel to the Swiss border. Machine guns, poison gas, and heavy artillery made short work of cavalry and massive frontal assaults by the infantry. As traditional methods of warfare failed, leaders turned to new technology to break the deadlock—tanks, poison gas, flame throwers, barbed wire, and submarines. All improved killing efficiency, but none proved decisive in ending the war of the trenches.

C. The German Offensive

The Schlieffen Plan had been dedicated to the principle that France could be swiftly eliminated. In that sense, the plan failed. German armies swept through Belgium but progressed more slowly than anticipated. Some German forces were siphoned off to the eastern front, in contradiction to Schlieffen's original strategy. At the critical moment when the Germans prepared to assault Paris, the German lines were weakened. Counterattacks by British and French forces halted the German advance at the Marne River. Trench lines established along the Marne to Ypres in Belgium remained little changed until the end of the war. With the failure of the Schlieffen Plan, Germany was committed to a two-front war.

D. War on the Eastern Front

The war on the eastern front was not limited to trench warfare because of the tremendous length of the lines dividing the Central Powers from Russia. Initially the Russians were able to take advantage of German strategy to advance into eastern Prussia, but the Germans swiftly met the threat. In 1914 the Germans won two devastating victories over Russian forces at the Tannenberg Forest and the Masurian Lakes. Thereafter the Russian armies enjoyed some success on the southern front against Austria-Hungary, but were constantly pressed back by the Germans. The inadequacy of the Russian transportation network made any military strategy requiring rapid movement of men and machines implausible. As the Russian armies suffered incredible losses (perhaps two million prisoners and casualties), it ceased to be a major force in the war effort.

E. War on the Western Front

War on the western front from the Battle of the Marne until 1917 consisted of a series of suicidal mass offensives, none of which succeeded in breaking the deadly cycle of trench warfare. The Germans launched the first offensive at Verdun. After ten months, the French lines held at a cost of over one million casualties to German and French forces. Verdun failed to convince the general staffs of the folly of mass frontal assault. The British attacked on the Somme, the French in the Champagne region, and the British again at Passchendaele.

F. War on the Periphery

Given the stalemate on the western front, the Allies attempted to open new fronts. Italy joined the war against Germany and Austria-Hungary in 1915, but failed to make much of an impact on the southern front in the Tyrol. Serbia was eliminated as an ally in the same year. The Allies attempted to open several fronts against the Ottoman Empire. The Gallipoli campaign in the Dardanelles was an unmitigated military disaster that ruined the early career of Winston Churchill, the administrator who proposed the strategy. British forces and their Arab allies were more successful in Egypt and Mesopotamia. Baghdad was captured in 1917. War on the seas was surprisingly indecisive. The British and German navies engaged in only one major battle, Jutland. German naval efforts after 1916 were limited to submarine warfare. Unrestricted use of submarines to assault seaborne commerce, even the ships of neutral nations, provoked international outrage. The British managed to limit the effectiveness of the German submarines through use of convoys, mines, and depth charges.

IV.   Adjusting to the Unexpected: Total War

A. Introduction

The First World War required the mobilization of entire national populations to support the war effort. The war imposed constitutional change, as governments controlled every aspect of economic life. The ability to maintain industrial production eventually decided the war's outcome.

B. Mobilizing The Home Front

As the war effort utilized most of the available men in the armed forces, women became increasingly responsible for industrial production. In all of the Allied countries, women became a significant factor in the production of weapons, food, and public services. Women even took over clerical positions in the military. After an early experiment with uncontrolled economies, all nations rapidly intervened to control the economy. In Germany, Walther Rathenau created government monopolies in sensitive industries. In Britain, production of munitions and weapons was under the supervision of a new administrative division, the Ministry of Munitions under Lloyd George. Governments were forced to divert food supplies to the armies and introduced food rationing at home. Even with rationing, the ravages of war produced food shortages in most Continental countries.

C. Silencing Dissent

Labor unrest and political opposition grew as the war continued without promise of victory. All countries experienced growing peace movements, especially among socialists. Governments responded by becoming more repressive. Censorship, emergency powers, and military rule became more common—even in previously liberal governments such as Britain's. Warring countries attempted to sponsor insurrection in the territories of their enemies. The Germans supported the Irish Easter Rebellion in 1916 against Britain. The Germans exported revolution to Russia by sending Lenin back to his home country in 1917. The British responded by supporting Zionism and fostering unrest among Jewish populations of the Central Powers. The British government also actively cooperated with Arab independence movements in the Ottoman Empire.

V.   The Russian Revolution and allied victory

A. Introduction

After three years of stalemate, there was a time of crisis for all combatants. Without dramatic victories and facing decreasing support on the home front, all nations looked for relief. In 1917 the course of the war was changed by Russian revolution and the entrance of the United States into the war.

B. Revolution in Russia

Russia was in the midst of an industrial revolution at the time of the outbreak of the First World War. As in all countries, industrialization caused social and economic dislocations. In 1905 Russian troops fired on labor demonstrators in Petrograd and initiated a revolution. After some reforms—the introduction of a national parliament, the Duma—the government returned to repressive measures to quell riots of laborers and peasants. Shut out of the government, workers united in independent labor organizations, the soviets. At the outset of the war, labor unrest resulted in numerous strikes. In order to fight the war, the tsar pressed industrial production at the expense of the agricultural economy. At the same time, he left the domestic government in the hands of his wife and a strange mystic, Rasputin. In March 1917 the workers' groups rebelled again. This time the tsar abdicated, leaving a vacuum of authority in Russia.

Power was divided between the workers' soviets, scattered throughout the cities of Russia, and the Duma, generally controlled by the small class of Russian bourgeoisie. The two groups could not cooperate. The situation was complicated by general rebellion among the peasants, who accepted the revolution and demanded grants of land. Disruption in the countryside led to aggravation of food shortages. Revolution also affected the Russian army. Constant defeats and horrendous losses sapped the will of the military. Many deserted or refused to fight, despite the decision of the Provisional Government to carry on the war. The overthrow of the tsar paved the way for the return of the exiled intelligentsia. Most influential of the returning intellectuals were the Marxist Social Democrats. The more moderate faction of the group, the Mensheviks, urged revisionism and cooperation with the Provisional Government and the Duma. The radicals, Lenin's Bolsheviks, demanded further revolution through the soviets. Lenin demanded an immediate end to the war, redistribution of land, and expansion of the revolution to the workers of western Europe. In July 1917 national demonstrations in favor of the soviets and against the Provisional Government were met with repression. As a partial sop to the demonstrators, Aleksandr Kerenski, a moderate socialist, was named to head the Provisional Government.

In November 1917 the Red Guards, the armed militia of the Petrograd soviet, seized the Russian capital. Members of the Provisional Government were either arrested or permitted to escape. All of the workers' soviets endorsed the overthrow and the leadership of Lenin.

Lenin immediately took Russia out of the war. In the treaty of Brest-Litovsk, the Russian leader accepted huge territorial losses to gain a peace settlement. So humiliating was the treaty that some Russian military officers refused to accept it. They launched a civil war against the soviet government. In order to fight the civil war, Lenin was also forced to narrow the base of government and institute a repressive dictatorship based on the authority of the secret police.

C. The United States enters the Great War

A friendly neutral throughout most of the war, the U.S. was drawn into the conflict as a result of German diplomatic blunders. Unrestricted submarine warfare, initiated in 1917, threatened American trade with Europe. The Germans also crudely attempted to lure the Mexican government into an alliance by offering the return of lands in the American Southwest. When the German plot became public in the Zimmermann telegram, President Woodrow Wilson sought and received a declaration of war. The United States' entry into the war shifted the manpower and war-materiel balance in favor of the Allies. Germany launched one last, desperate offensive in 1918. Despite early success, the German attack failed to reach Paris. The weight of Allied arms, reinforced by the arrival of increasing numbers of Americans, forced the Germans to withdraw. Rather than allow the war to be taken to German soil, the German general staff signed an armistice on 11 November 1918.

V.   Settling the Peace

A. Introduction

The peace negotiations were designed to restore stability to all of Europe. Outside the negotiations, but casting a shadow over the deliberations, was revolutionary Russia.

B. Wilson's Fourteen Points

The peace settlement was a compromise. President Woodrow Wilson of the United States represented the prewar, liberal view of international relations. His proposals were embodied in the Fourteen Points, which included open diplomacy instead of secret alliances, a return to freedom of trade and commerce, reduction of national armaments, and an international organization of states to oversee the peace. The latter provision was ironically accepted in Europe where the League of Nations became a reality, but rejected by the Congress of the United States who refused to become a member of the new organization. Georges Clemenceau of France represented the paranoid, war-weary view of the other Allies. He demanded the creation of buffer states to surround Germany, much as France was surrounded after the Napoleonic Wars. While few changes were made in the national boundaries of western Europe, the map of eastern Europe was totally redrawn.

C. Treaties and Territories

While few changes were made in the national boundaries of western Europe, the map of eastern Europe was totally redrawn. In the Middle East the British issued the Balfour declaration giving support for a Jewish homeland in Palestine while promising independence to the Arabic speaking people. In the end the Middle East was carved up and divided among the European powers. New states were carved out in Finland, Latvia, Estonia, Lithuania, Poland, Czechoslovakia, Austria, Hungary, and Yugoslavia. Finally, the Treaty of Versailles introduced the War Guilt Clause, a statement fixing blame for the war on Germany and requiring the payment of reparations to the victorious Allies. Germany was economically crippled. The peace settlement was weakened by the exclusion of Russia from the negotiating table, by the refusal of the United States Congress to endorse all aspects of the treaty, and by a growing desire for isolation in Great Britain.

TIMELINE

Insert the following events into the timeline. This should help you to compare important historical events chronologically.

Bloody Sunday in St. Petersburg   assassination of Archduke Ferdinand
Treaty of Versailles signed   German offensive at Verdun
Russia signs Treaty of Brest-Litovsk   Bolsheviks seize control of Russian government

1905	
1914	
1916	
1917	
1918	
1919	

TERMS, PEOPLE, EVENTS

The following terms, people, and events are important to your understanding of the chapter. Define each one.

Schlieffen Plan	Plan XVII	Gavrilo Princip
Archduke Franz Ferdinand	Allies	Central Powers
trench warfare	poison gas	unrestricted submarine warfare
first battle of the Marne	battle of Tannenberg	battle of the Masurian Lakes
Verdun	the Somme	Passchendaele offensive
Gallipoli	battle of Jutland	Total war
Walther Rathenau	Lloyd George	V. I. Lenin
Balfour Declaration	*Lusitania*	Zimmermann telegram
Ludendorff offensive	armistice American	Expeditionary Forces
Great War	Council of Four	Fourteen Points
League of Nations	Georges Clemenceau	Treaty of Versailles
Reparations	Bloody Sunday	Duma
Soviets	Prince Georgi Lvov	Aleksandr Kerenski
Provisional Government	Petrograd Soviet	Social Democrats
Mensheviks	Bolsheviks	April Theses
Leon Trotsky	Red Guards	Treaty of Brest-Litovsk

MAP EXERCISE

The following exercise is intended to clarify the geophysical environment and the spatial relationships among the important objects and places mentioned in the chapter.

1. In what sense did the Treaty of Versailles restore the situation in central Europe that existed prior to the unification of Germany in 1870?

2. Locate the following places on the map.

    the western front   the eastern Front
    the Allies   the Central Powers

3. Identify all those nations created as a result of the Treaty of Versailles.

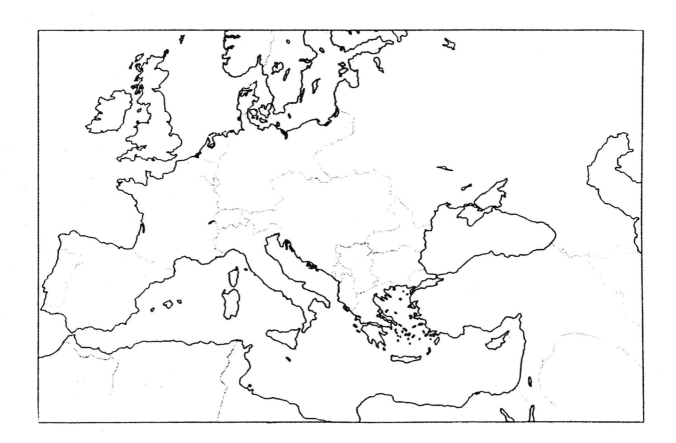

MAKING CONNECTIONS

The following questions are intended to emphasize important ideas within the chapter.

1. How did the system of alliances at the beginning of the twentieth century actually contribute to the outbreak of World War I? How did military strategies assist in the failure of peace?

2. What factors contributed to the creation of a military stalemate on the western front? How did the eastern front differ from the western front? Why did both the Central Powers and the Allies turn to warfare outside Europe?

3. Define "total war." How did governments organize to handle the concept of total war?

4. What caused the United States to enter World War I? What impact did the entry of the United States have on the outcome of the war?

5. What were the terms of the Treaty of Versailles? What were the implications of the treaty on future political stability in Europe?

6. What led to the tsar's abdication? What centers of authority existed in the absence of authoritarian rule? How did the Bolsheviks seize power?

PUTTING LARGER CONCEPTS TOGETHER

The following questions test your ability to summarize the major conclusions of the chapter.

1. In many ways the Great War can be said to have destroyed the liberal consciousness of Europe. Considering the means by which the war was fought, the policies necessary to wage total war, and the peace negotiations that followed the end of the conflict, why was the basis for liberalism eroded?

2. Was World War I the necessary aftermath of the centralization of political authority in central Europe after 1870? How did the peace settlement seek to deal with the question of central Europe?

SELF-TEST OF FACTUAL INFORMATION

1. While alliances based on military support did NOT cause the outbreak of World War I, they did

    a. generate an atmosphere of economic control and effectively ended all free-trade market economies.
    b. permit weak nations to act irresponsibly with the certainty that they would be defended by more powerful partners.
    c. divide Europe into seven balanced alliance systems likely to come into conflict.
    d. effectively terminate the idea of "free will" within the national communities of western Europe.

2. The German plan intended to bring World War I to a swift conclusion was

    a. the Schlieffen Plan.
    b. Plan XVII.
    c. the Maginot Plan.
    d. the Ludendorff offensive.

3. Which of the following best describes the performance of the Russian armies on the eastern front?

    a. The tsarist forces fought with enthusiasm and tenacity against the Germans but met their match in battle with the Austrians.
    b. Despite being provided with state-of-the-art weapons, Russian soldiers refused to fight.
    c. After initial victories against the Austrians, the Russian army was literally bled to death due to poor planning and poor leadership.
    d. In desperate hand-to-hand combat, Russian soldiers distinguished themselves against superior numbers of English, French, and Serb soldiers.

4. Britain's effort to open up a third front in southern Europe was the

    a. Passchendaele offensive.
    b. Gallipoli campaign.
    c. Verdun offensive.
    d. Boer War.

5. Which of the following was NOT a factor leading to food shortages in Europe during World War I?

   a. The need for large numbers of soldiers at the front pulled men away from agricultural production.
   b. Fear of requisitioning and the general uncertainties of the war caused agricultural producers to hoard supplies.
   c. The United States remained firmly neutral and cut off all food supplies to Europe.
   d. The European enemies successfully targeted trade routes and limited imports of food.

6. Which of the following statements concerning the entry of the United States into World War I is NOT accurate?

   a. U.S. naval power contributed to large convoys used to protect Allied shipping.
   b. Unlike the European nations, the U.S. never created a wartime bureaucracy for the management of the war.
   c. The U.S. sent tens of thousands of conscript fighting men to serve in Europe.
   d. The entry of the U.S. altered the nature of European politics by incorporating the U.S. into future deliberations.

7. All the following nations were excluded from the peace conference following World War I EXCEPT

   a. Germany.
   b. Austria-Hungary.
   c. Soviet Russia.
   d. Japan.

8. In response to Bloody Sunday, the tsar

   a. abdicated in 1905.
   b. legalized political parties and established the Duma.
   c. passed massive legislation intended to ease the plight of the peasantry.
   d. turned most aspects of government over to the soviets.

9. V. I. Lenin was

   a. the leader of the Menshevik faction of the Russian Social Democrats.
   b. committed to the principle of a cadre of professional politicians and revolutionaries who would lead others in the overthrow of capitalism.
   c. committed to continuation of Russian participation in World War I.
   d. in favor of delaying the revolution and cooperation with the Provisional Government.

10. Which of the following countries did NOT occupy parts of Russia after the end of World War I?

    a. England and France
    b. United States
    c. Austria-Hungary
    d. Japan

CHAPTER 27

The European Search for Stability, 1920-1939

OUTLINE

I.   The Hard Lessons of Inflation

In the period after World War I, inflation struck the economies of Europe and the United States. Hardest hit were Germany and the states of eastern Europe. Inflation in Germany actually began during the war, when the imperial government funded the military by printing additional supplies of money. The terms of Versailles and demands for reparation further damaged German currency. The Weimar government also printed money, until basic supplies and food literally cost cartloads of paper notes to buy. German citizens blamed their own government. Radical political groups gained popularity by scapegoating the democratic system, ethnic minorities, and Jews. Inflation and economic hardship produced political extremism.

II.   Geographical Tour: Europe after 1918

  A. Introduction

Despite the Marxist expectations for a universal capitalist collapse, the years after World War I saw the survival of governments in western Europe. The United States, the savior of the Allied cause in the war, withdrew from active participation except on its own economic terms. The other giant, Russia, was isolated from European affairs in order to quarantine the spread of socialist revolution.

  B. New Nation-States, New Problems

Eastern Europe was most changed by the peace treaties that ended the Great War. New nations created in 1919 hemmed in the Russian menace. Unfortunately, the new states were extremely unstable. Ethnic minorities within the newly formed states demanded recognition. Eastern Europe was generally behind in industrialization. The end of the Great War did nothing to improve economic prospects in the region. Geography dictated that most of the new nations were more dependent on Germany than on western Europe. Finally, the eastern states feuded among themselves and their more ancient neighbors over boundaries. Germany and Russia were intent on recovering territories lost as a result of peace negotiations.

  C. German Recovery

Germany was defeated but not destroyed. The war had not been carried to its territory. New states in central Europe were susceptible to German economic and diplomatic influence. German losses were limited to its western boundaries and the "corridor" ceded to Prussia. German foreign policy in the decades after 1919 was predicated on recovering lost territory on the French border and in the Polish Corridor. German economic development required discovering new markets. Initially, attempts were made to open trade with Russia. When the Russian economy proved unable to absorb the products of German industry, Germany turned to Britain, France, and the United States. Under foreign minister Gustav Stresemann, Germany sought to heal past grievances and revise the most economically damaging aspects of the Treaty of Versailles. The new sense of cooperation was reflected in a series of non-aggression treaties signed at Locarno in 1925. At the same time, Germany rearmed secretly in contradiction of the "spirit of Locarno" to regain its dominant position in central Europe.

D. France's Search for Security

France desperately needed to maintain its military advantage over demilitarized Germany. When Britain and the United States refused to extend the alliances created in the First World War, France created new ties with the new nations of eastern Europe—Poland, Czechoslovakia, Romania, and Yugoslavia. Committed to the strict enforcement of the Versailles Treaty against Germany, the French armies actually entered the Ruhr district of Germany in 1923 in order to force payment of reparations. In 1925 France was forced to reverse its strict observation of the Treaty of Versailles and joined the negotiations at Locarno. French foreign policy continued to distrust German intentions even after Locarno. In the late 1920s France began construction of an elaborate series of defenses along the German border, the Maginot line.

E. The United States in Europe

After the Great War, no balance of power could be maintained in Europe without the active participation of the United States. The government of the United States shrank from the task. With only the USSR (a member in 1934) and Germany (a member in 1926), the United States remained outside the League of Nations. By remaining aloof, the United States denied the League any real authority as a peace-keeping force. U.S. policy in Europe was dedicated to restoring German economic vitality. The U.S. also actively supported the Kellogg-Briand Pact of 1928, which renounced war as a means of resolving diplomatic problems.

III.   Crisis and Collapse in a World Economy

A. Introduction

At the end of the war all the belligerents owed large sums of money which they borrowed first from their own population to finance the enormous expense of the Great War.

B. International Loans and Trade Barriers

In additional to the sale of bonds to their own citizens, the Governments also borrowed from other nations and when that was not enough, the governments simply printed paper money with nothing to back it up. The result was inflation. The greatest creditor nation after 1919 was the United States. The U.S. did not want to accept payment in the inflated post-war European currencies, but had difficulty making any other sort of arrangement. The Allies other than the U.S. counted on German reparation payments to restore their economies and pay the war debt. The amount of reparations was unreasonable. Neither the Allies nor the Germans believed it could be paid in full. In Germany the payment of reparations was viewed as an international disgrace. When Germany fell behind in reparations, France fell behind in repaying loans from the United States. To force Germany to pay, France invaded the German Ruhr, an important industrial center. The Germans responded with passive resistance supported by payments of paper currency to the unemployed German laborers. Rampant inflation weakened the German mark and threatened international financial chaos. To restore equilibrium, Charles Dawes, an American banker, urged reduction in German repayments and an American loan to temporarily prime the German economy. France was bullied into accepting the plan by threats of withdrawal of American financial support. All countries saw trade as a means of accumulating income to pay debts and restore the total European economy. In order to be successful, the restoration of trade had to be based on open markets and stable currency. The policy of the United States frustrated plans for restoring European markets to prewar conditions. The U.S. insisted on protecting domestic production with high tariffs that shut out European producers. The U.S. also found its own products too expensive for European consumers because of inflation and unstable currencies. Even with enormous infusions of American cash, Germany continued to resent the reparations. Despite difficulties, most countries prospered in the postwar era. Prosperity was largely illusory, however. American protectionism, German anger over reparations, irresponsible speculation in stocks, and low long-term capital investment led to the disaster of 1929.

C. The Great Depression

The American stock market crash of 1929 signaled a worldwide depression. Except for nonindustrialized nations and the isolated Soviet economy, the financial and economic systems of the world economy collapsed. Depression in the United States meant an end to American capital in Europe, without which most countries could not survive. In 1931 Great Britain was forced to renounce the gold standard, a decision that amounted to ceding that country's preeminent position in finance. Faith in a self-correcting economy evaporated with dramatic effects on liberal governments. Throughout the world, political change followed the footsteps of depression.

IV.   The Soviet Union's Separate Path

A. Introduction

Soviet Russia was forced to embark on a program of rapid industrialization with drastic costs to Russian society.

B. The Soviet Regime at the End of the Civil War

The Great War followed immediately by the civil wars after the Russian Revolution devastated the Russian industrial and agricultural economy. The hold of the Bolsheviks over the government was in doubt. The government was directed by the Politburo, a seven-man committee of Bolsheviks, who undertook stabilization of the Russian economy. The first step was the declaration of a planned national economy, favored by Politburo member Leon Trotsky, as opposed to a free market economy. Trotsky actually argued for the militarization of all labor, but Lenin, while accepting the temporary necessity of a state-run economy, wanted to retain the autonomy of the labor unions.

C. The New Economic Policy, 1921-1928

The New Economic Policy, or NEP, was defined in the summer of 1921. It abolished requisition of agricultural products in favor of peasant payment of a percentage of production to the state. Surpluses could be disposed of on private markets. The task of industrialization was taken on by Nikolai Bukharin, another Politburo member. Bukharin counted on a prosperous agricultural sector and foreign investment to create the necessary capital for industry. Peasant profits would create demand for Russian manufactured goods. The earliest stages of the NEP seemed to promise a successful compromise between controlled socialism and the free market. To some communists, the NEP seemed too capitalistic, particularly in its support of a market economy for agriculture. When Lenin died in 1924, a division in the Party occurred over the nature of economic planning. In 1928 Joseph Stalin, general secretary of the Communist Party, intervened in the agricultural economy when peasants attempted to hoard their produce. Stalin played on political fears of internal and external attack in order to justify closing down the free market for agricultural produce. Both Trotsky and Bukharin, whose reputations were made by the NEP, were dismissed from the Politburo. Both were eventually killed.

D. Stalin's Rise to Power

Stalin was born into a poverty stricken family in Georgia (province of the Russian Empire). As a teenager he joined the Marxist movement and became a follower of Lenin. Stalin ruled Russia as a dictator from 1928 to 1953. From the outset of the socialist revolution in Russia, Stalin had served as a political expert, particularly with respect to ethnic minorities. Stalin created a political cult of Leninism and played carefully on his relationship to Lenin as a means of building his own political identity. At the same time, Stalin ruthlessly eliminated his political rivals.

E. The First Five-Year Plan

Stalin committed Russia to a program of rapid industrialization to be based on wringing all profits from agriculture. The NEP and its former leaders were cast aside in favor of Stalin's Five-Year Plan. Heavy industries were targeted for growth. A workforce was created out of peasant men and women. Free markets in the agricultural sector were replaced with the policy of collectivization—confiscating all private land and establishing state farms. By 1938 private land was virtually eliminated. Millions of peasants died, and peasant society was destroyed. At a cost, a totally state-planned economy was created.

F. The Comintern, Economic Development, and the Purges

When socialist revolutions failed to occur in western Europe, the Soviet Union began to revise its diplomacy and seek recognition in the West. By 1924 all countries but the United States recognized the Soviet government. U.S. recognition came in 1933. Marxist movements throughout the world were subjugated to the Russian Communist Party. The Comintern was based in Moscow and consisted of representatives of thirty-seven countries. Until 1929 the Comintern also cooperated with other, non-Marxist socialist parties in a "common front." Stalin withdrew support for non-communist groups in 1929, thus splitting socialism in Europe. Stalin's second Five-Year Plan continued to emphasize heavy industries and agricultural collectivization. The continued development of heavy industrial capacity advanced Russian production of armaments. Stalin secured his own position as dictator by liquidating all enemies in the Great Purge. Perhaps as many as 300,000 people died in Stalin's purges between 1934 and 1938.

G. Women and the Family in the New Soviet State

Initially, the Soviet state pledged to emancipate women (achieved in 1917) and to raise them to equal status with Russian males. Despite appearances, Russian women suffered after the Revolution. During the NEP, industries were slow to hire women because of liberal provisions for child care and maternity leaves. Women failed to enter the top echelons of the Communist Party. The traditional role of women as mothers was officially reinstated as a result of declining birth rates. After 1936, abortion was illegal and women were expected to perform the dual roles of mother and worker. The amount of labor imposed on women actually increased as a result.

V. The Rise of Fascist Dictatorship in Italy

A. Introduction

Rooted in the mass political movements of the late nineteenth century, right-wing movements sought to fill the void between the discredited liberalism of prewar Europe and the revolutionary socialism of the Soviet Union and radical socialism. Committed to extreme nationalism and the politics of the irrational, fascism became a powerful force in post-war politics.

B. Mussolini's Italy

Benito Mussolini was a former socialist and war veteran. In the 1920s he formed a new political organization, the Fascists, and launched an attack on the chaotic parliamentary government of Italy. Mussolini created a staunchly nationalistic party that identified communists, big business, and labor unions as enemies of the Italian state. Embraced by a middle class seeking any kind of security in the shaky postwar economy, Mussolini's Fascists began to take over Italian cities, including Rome in 1922. Mussolini neutralized his political rivals through use of violence and terrorism. By 1925 Mussolini's party controlled the government entirely as a one-party dictatorship. Once in power, Mussolini concocted a strange alliance with big business to create the "corporate" state. The dictator was also able to come to an accommodation with the other power of Italy, Pope Pius XI. The pope agreed to the Lateran Treaty which recognized the continued role of Catholicism in marriage laws and education. In return, the Vatican was recognized as a sovereign state.

C. Mussolini's Plans for Empire

Mussolini's corporativist state failed to solve the problems of the depression. To focus popular opinion away from economic failures, Mussolini committed Italy to an imperialist scheme in northern Africa. In 1935 Italian troops invaded Ethiopia. The League of Nations was unable to prevent Italian occupation of Ethiopia, although Britain and France expressed their displeasure. Mussolini turned to an alliance with fascist Germany, the Pact of Steel, in 1936. In 1938, Italy annexed Albania.

V.   Hitler and the Third Reich

A. Introduction

Between 1924 and 1929, inflation increased despite the growing economy in Germany. The unsteady economic mood was reflected in the political party system in the Weimar Republic. The depression of 1929 destroyed German prosperity. American loans were withdrawn, reparations could not be paid, and the welfare system could not be funded. The volatile party system destroyed parliamentary effectiveness. In the wake of economic disaster, the Weimar constitution was overthrown.

B. Hitler's Rise to Power

Adolf Hitler was, like Mussolini, a military veteran of the First World War. A believer in the betrayal of the German military, Hitler blamed the Weimar Republic in general and Jews and communists in particular for Germany's defeat in 1919. Hitler's message was particularly attractive to German military veterans who believed in the myth of the Weimar "stab in the back." Hitler's first attempt at political revolution in Mussolini's style, the Munich Beer Hall Putsch of 1923, was halted by military force. Hitler served a brief jail term during which he wrote *Mein Kampf*, a right-wing diatribe against Jews, communists, and middle-class liberals whom Hitler blamed for the downfall of Germany.

Hitler changed his tactics after the abortive Putsch and began to seek power within the constitutional party system. By 1928, the National Socialists were a small, but recognizable party in German politics. In 1933 Adolf Hitler, as leader of the largest single party in the Weimar Republic, was offered the position of Chancellor by President Paul von Hindenburg. Hitler immediately declared a national emergency on the pretext of socialist threat and imposed a legal dictatorship. The Nazis abolished political parties, imposed censorship, outlawed labor unions, and suspended parliamentary government. Hitler used violence administered by paramilitary organizations to gradually centralize his authority. The first of the paramilitary groups was the SA (*Sturmabteilung*) headed by Ernst Rohm. Rohm was eliminated by Heinrich Himmler, head of the SS (*Shutzstaffel*) in 1934. The SS then emerged as the chief enforcement arm of the Nazi government.

C. Nazi Goals

Hitler's goals were territorial expansion (*Lebensraum*), economic recovery, and rearmament. Hitler wanted world domination for Germany, but established control of central and eastern Europe as his immediate goal. Hitler devoted an enormous proportion of Germany's income to creating a powerful military. In order to provide for military self-sufficiency, Hitler promoted the concept of autarky, production of all materials needed for the military machine. Armament industries and other state-supported businesses created full employment in Germany. When it appeared that Germany could not achieve autarky, Hitler determined it was necessary to conquer nations that had supplies of natural resources.

D. Propaganda, Racism, and Culture

Joseph Goebbels headed the Ministry of Propaganda, which organized massive displays of public loyalty to the Nazi regime. The Nazis created party organizations for children of both sexes. Women were urged to stop working, get married, and have children. In 1939 when the outbreak of war caused labor shortages, the Nazis urged women to return to the workforce. By 1943 German women were conscripted for labor duty. To secure political unanimity, the Nazis taught the doctrine of racial purity. Foreigners, communists, homosexuals, the mentally ill, and gypsies were all targeted for expulsion, euthanasia, or persecution; but no group received the degree of persecution reserved for Jews. On 9 November 1938, widespread destruction of Jewish property was carried out during *Kristallnacht*. Mandatory sterilization of "undesirables" was required to prevent the dissipation of pure, German breeding lines.

VI. Democracies in Crisis

A. Introduction

The leaders of Europe's democracies made only tentative steps to respond to the Great Depression. As a result, internal dissension and political disruption were common.

B. The Failure of the Left in France

Paralyzed by the multiplicity of political parties, the Third Republic of France took virtually no action to ameliorate the conditions of the depression. In 1936 demands for change led to the victory of a socialist government, the Popular Front, under Leon Blum. Although it promised reforms—wage increases, paid vacations, and collective bargaining—the Popular Front was unable to deliver on its campaign promises. Blum's government was voted out in 1937. The failure of socialist politics led to the formation of right-wing groups that favored Hitler over Blum. Leftwing parties drifted ever farther in the political spectrum into communism. French politics remained fragmented, but became more ideologically radical.

C. Muddling Through in Great Britain

The depression forced the establishment of a coalition government in Britain. The Labour government of Ramsay MacDonald resigned, although MacDonald remained prime minister. He was joined by members of the Liberal and the Conservative Parties in forming the National Government (1931-1935). The National Government took Britain off the gold standard, resurrected tariffs, and established state-planned production quotas for industry. Sir Oswald Mosley, favored imperial development as the solution for British economic problems. When his advice was refused, Mosley formed the British Union of Fascists. John Maynard Keynes urged more vigorous government intervention. Despite initial success, the BUF was declared illegal in 1936 and rejected by the majority of Englishmen. Although the National Government failed to deal aggressively with the depression, the British tradition of liberal, parliamentary government emerged unscathed.

D. The Spanish Republic as Battleground

Spain became a republic in 1931 and rapidly formed a socialist government, the National Front, that revolutionized the traditional Spanish economy. The directness of the assault on the aristocracy, the Catholic Church, and the military resulted in civil war. Republicans (supporters of the Spanish Popular Front) confronted Nationalists (monarchists, Church supporters, and the military). Germany and Italy intervened on the side of the Nationalists under Francisco Franco. The Soviet Union supported the socialist Republicans. Unofficial international brigades, manned primarily by communists, volunteered in support of the Republic. Franco's Nationalist armies won a bitter victory in 1939.

TIMELINE

Insert the following events into the timeline. This should help you to compare important historical events chronologically.

beginning of NEP in Russia   Stalin initiates Great Purge in Soviet Union
Hitler becomes Chancellor of Germany   Great Depression begins
Spanish Civil War begins   Fascists achieve parliamentary majority in Italy

1921	
1924	
1929	
1933	
1934	
1936	

TERMS, PEOPLE, EVENTS

The following terms, people, and events are important to your understanding of the chapter. Define each one.

Treaty of Rapallo	Gustav Stresemann	spirit of Locarno
Ruhr	League of Nations	Kellogg-Briand Pact
Dawes Plan	Young Plan	Great Depression
Smoot-Hawley Tariff	Leon Ttotsky	Joseph Stalin
Nikolai Bukharin	New Economic Policy	First Five-Year Plan
Kulaks	collectivization	Comintern
Second Five-Year Plan	Great Purge	fascism
Benito Mussolini	March on Rome	Lateran Treaty
Rome-Berlin Axis	Pact of Steel	Adolf Hitler
Beer Hall Putsch	*Mein Kampf*	Third Reich
Ernst Rohm	Heinrich Himmler	SS
SA	*Lebensraum*	autarky
Joseph Goebbels	Hitler Youth	*Kristallnacht*
Third Republic in France	Leon Blum	Popular Front in France
Ramsay MacDonald	National Government	Sir Oswald Mosley
Popular Front in Spain	Spanish Civil War	General Francisco Franco
Fascism	Weimar Republic	Nazism

MAP EXERCISE

The following exercise is intended to clarify the geophysical environment and the spatial relationships among the important objects and places mentioned in the chapter.

1. In what sense did the failure of democracies reflect the destabilization of central Europe following World War I? [See Map Exercise, Chapter 26.]

2. Locate the following places on the map.

    Identify the fascist states of Europe.
    Identify the democracies after 1940.

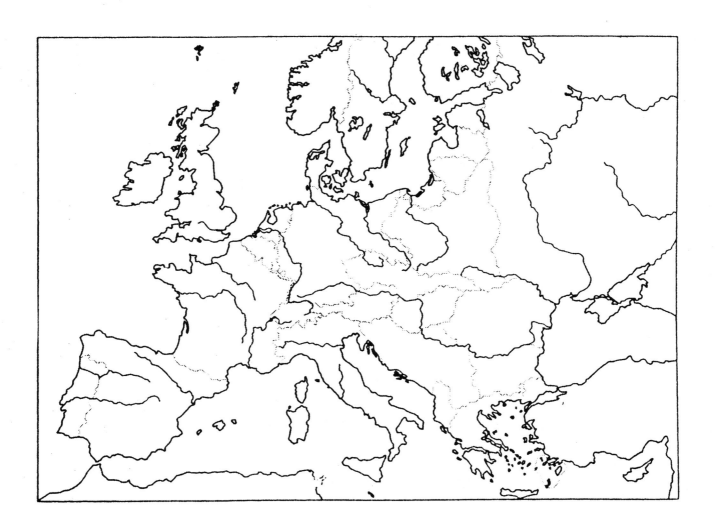

MAKING CONNECTIONS

The following questions are intended to emphasize important ideas within the chapter.

1. What were the problems leading to political instability in east central Europe after World War I? To what extent was Germany able to recover? What were France's primary economic and political concerns? What was the impact of the U.S. on the diplomatic and economic situation in Europe?

2. What were the causes of the economic crisis in Europe? What attempts were made to forestall disaster? What was the Great Depression?

3. What political and economic decisions did Lenin make after 1920? How was the New Economic Plan supposed to work?

4. How did Stalin achieve power? How did Stalin redefine the political and economic structure of the Soviet Union? What was the position of women within the Soviet social and economic system?

5. How did democracies fare between 1920 and 1940? Define fascism.

6. How did Benito Mussolini achieve power? What was the nature of the Italian fascist state? What plans for expansion did Mussolini have?

7. Why did the Weimar Republic fail? How did Adolf Hitler achieve power? What sort of state did Hitler establish in the Third Reich? What were Hitler's social and economic goals? How were they related to German expansion?

8. Describe the types of government established in France, Britain, and Spain in the aftermath of the Great Depression? How successful were these governments in meeting social, economic, and political challenges?

PUTTING LARGER CONCEPTS TOGETHER

The following questions test your ability to summarize the major conclusions of the chapter.

1. What caused the rise of dictatorships in Europe following World War I? Consider the possible effects of the Treaty of Versailles, the Great Depression, and the withdrawal system that developed after 1920.

2. Were the dictatorships more successful in dealing with the social, economic, and political crises that arose after 1920? Why or why not?

SELF-TEST OF FACTUAL INFORMATION

1. Which of the following was NOT a factor in the political destabilization of the new nations of east central Europe?

   a. ethnic diversity within the new boundaries
   b. borders that made little economic sense
   c. attempts by the new nations to expand their borders at the expense of their neighbors
   d. France's attempts to restore the pre-World War I borders

2. The German foreign minister who was responsible for the attempts to restore conciliatory policies toward France and England during the Weimar Republic was

   a. Aristide Briand.
   b. Gustav Stresemann.
   c. Ernst Rohm.
   d. Walter Gropius.

3. The Dawes Plan

   a. eliminated the German reparation payments.
   b. turned the Ruhr over to France in lieu of German reparation payments.
   c. gave Germany a more realistic payment schedule for reparations and extended American credit.
   d. opened American markets to free trade with Europe.

4. Which of the following men was NOT a major factor in the early Soviet Politburo?

   a. Leon Trotsky
   b. Nikolai Bukharin
   c. Joseph Stalin
   d. Yuri Andropov

5. Which of the following statements about Stalin's Five-Year Plans is most accurate?

   a. They resulted in a freer marketplace for Soviet products.
   b. Their goal was to squeeze profits out of the agricultural sector in order to fund industrialization.
   c. They handed direction of the Soviet economy over to the kulaks.
   d. They deferred the process of collectivization to a later period.

6. Which of the following statements concerning fascism is NOT accurate?

    a. Fascists employed revolutionary language similar to that of the Left.
    b. Fascism was ultranationalist, and the use of force was central to its appeal.
    c. Fascists supported the capitalist economy and liberal political institutions and values.
    d. Fascists condemned socialists.

7. In the Lateran Treaty, Mussolini

    a. absorbed the papal estates into the state of Italy.
    b. forced the papacy to recognize Adolf Hitler's fascist government in Germany.
    c. recognized papal sovereignty in the Vatican and around St. Peter's Basilica.
    d. withdrew the Catholic Church's monopoly over education and the Italian marriage laws.

8. Hitler became chancellor of Germany

    a. as a result of the Beer Hall Putsch.
    b. by conducting a military overthrow of the Weimar Republic.
    c. after achieving a majority within the Weimar Reichstag.
    d. when the president of the Republic invited him to form a government.

9. Hitler's economic program of self-sufficiency was called an

    a. Lebensraum.
    b. autarky.
    c. Kristalluacht.
    d. Mein Kampf.

10. In what European country did the election of a radical Popular Front government lead to civil war?

    a. Spain
    b. France
    c. Britain
    d. Belgium

CHAPTER 28

Global Conflagration: World War II, 1939-1945

OUTLINE

I.   Precursor of War

By 1938, Hitler was firmly in control of Germany. In March of 1938 he annexed Austria to Germany. Afterward he set out to remove the remaining obstacles to German control of Eastern Europe — Czechoslovakia and Poland.

II.   Aggression and Conquest

A. Introduction

The other states of Europe and the United States failed to take action prior to 1939 to halt aggression. Both Germany in Europe and Japan in China took advantage of the opportunity to seize territories belonging to other nations.

B. Hitler's Foreign Policy and Appeasement

Hitler openly rearmed Germany, withdrew from the League of Nations, and ignored the provisions of the Treaty of Versailles. In 1938 he annexed Austria to Germany and threatened Czechoslovakia on the pretext of protecting the German minority in the Sudetenland. Neither France nor Britain were willing to risk war to defend Czechoslovakia. Prime Minister Neville Chamberlain of Britain offered to yield the Sudetenland to Hitler in return for promises of peace. When Hitler increased his demands, Chamberlain and the Prime Ministers of France and Italy met with Hitler at Munich. At the Munich conference, Chamberlain's policy of appeasement avoided war by granting Germany's requirements for peace. Shortly thereafter, Hitler's armies occupied all of Czechoslovakia. He then began pressuring Poland to surrender the Polish corridor.

C. Hitler's War, 1939-1941

Hitler prepared the way for war in western Europe by concluding alliances with Italy and the Soviet Union. Britain and France recognized that Hitler intended to continue military expansion and signed an alliance in 1939 to defend Poland. In the month of September 1939, Poland fell to advancing German armies. Just before the Polish collapse, the Soviet Union also invaded. Stalin's armies also swallowed up the Baltic States and defeated Finland by 1940. The invasion of Poland at last brought both France and Britain into the war against fascism. During the winter of 1939, there were no offensives. In 1940 the German armies launched *Blitzkrieg* attacks against Denmark, Norway, the Netherlands, Belgium, and Luxembourg. The mobile German *Panzer* units then swept through northern France against a demoralized French army. In June 1940 the French surrendered. France was divided into two parts: the north directly governed by the Germans in Paris, and the south governed by a collaborationist government at Vichy under Marshal Petain. The collapse of France left Britain alone against the German attack. The German air force, the air force (*Luftwaffe*), began saturation bombing of English cities. Under the leadership of Winston Churchill, the prime minister, the British survived and denied the Germans air superiority in the Battle of Britain. The Germans decided against an amphibious invasion of the island. In the Balkans, Hitler's forces took advantage of a military coup and ethnic divisions to seize Yugoslavia. From Yugoslavia they mounted a successful attack on Greece. Control of the Balkans provided the Germans with food supplies and invaluable petroleum resources. German control of southeastern Europe also threatened British supply routes to Egypt and the southern regions of the Soviet Union.

D. Collaboration and Resistance

Governments of subject states were ruled by collaborators who cooperated with Germany because of fear of communism, potential opportunity to regain lands lost in the Treaty of Versailles, of promises of independence, or simply to mitigate the impact of the Nazi occupation. Resistance to Nazi occupation was widespread. After the German attack on Russia in 1941, many communists throughout Europe took active measures against the Germans. The most successful was Josip Broz of Yugoslavia, known as Tito, but in general the actions of resistance movements were ineffective against German military power.

III. Racism and Destruction

A. Introduction

Both the Germans and the Japanese made use of spurious scientific theories to justify slaughter of groups they determined to be inferior to the master races. They were not alone. The United States interned Japanese-American citizens on the basis of racial stereotypes.

B. Enforcing Nazi Racial Policies

The Nazis identified various groups as racially and genetically inferior. Gypsies were subjected to discriminatory legislation, removed to internment camps, and systematically slaughtered during the war. The Nazi state discriminated against children of racially mixed marriages and provided for the euthanasia of "defective" people—the mentally ill and those with physical defects. All types of conditions were considered hereditary and capable of polluting the German population. The state provided for the compulsory sterilization of the homeless, criminals, alcoholics, and prostitutes. Homosexuality was punishable by castration or internment in concentration camps.

C. The Destruction of Europe's Jews

German policies against the Jews evolved gradually. After *Kristallnacht*, Jewish property was confiscated and Jews were confined to ghettoes within the cities of Germany and Poland. Mass murder of Slavs and Jews began following the invasion of Poland. During the invasion of Russia, German troops competed to demonstrate efficiency in murdering the inferior Slavic peoples. Heinrich Himmler of the SS suggested that poison gas would be more efficient as a killing mechanism than the mass shooting of prisoners and noncombatants. In 1941 a network of death camps was constructed to carry out the "Final Solution." The death camps targeted Jews, Slavs, homosexuals, and the political enemies of the Third Reich. As many as eleven million men, women, and children suffered under the most inhumane conditions prior to mass execution. The most horrible of the death camps was Auschwitz in Poland. The sick and aged were immediately dispatched to the gas chambers, while the young were sent to work until disease, starvation, or exhaustion made them unfit for the duties assigned them. The Jewish population could offer no effective resistance to extermination. They were locked in a country that universally accepted their fate and by immigration policies established in nearly all nations that made it impossible for them to leave. Even the United States and Palestine refused emigrants from Europe. Few Jews understood the final fate of those who were arrested. When the Warsaw ghetto attempted militant resistance, they were liquidated by the German army. Generally speaking, all governments were aware of the German policy of extermination. Collaborationist governments occasionally assisted with rounding up Jews and minorities. Britain and the United States simply ignored the plight of the victims of the slaughter. The Holocaust represented systematic extermination of eleven million people of which six million were Jews.

IV.   Allied Victory

A. Introduction

In the spring of 1941, Hitler controlled the continent of Europe and was allied with the Soviet Union, Italy, and Japan in what seemed an indomitable Axis. In the summer of 1941, the war changed, Germany invaded Russia, and in December Japan bombed the American fleet at Pearl Harbor. Germany now faced the alliance of the United States, Britain and the Soviet Union with their inexhaustible resources.

B. The Soviet Union's Great Patriotic War

With the Western countries neutralized, Hitler felt free in 1941 to carry his war against communism to the Soviet Union. Stalin, unprepared for a German invasion, called for an alliance with Britain and the United States. Operation Barbarossa, as the German invasion was called, swept through western Russia to the outskirts of Moscow. There a determined defense and the Russian winter put an end to the blitzkrieg. In December 1941, the Russian armies under General Zhukov counterattacked. Losses on both sides were enormous, but the German forces on the eastern front were crushed. In the following year, Hitler ordered a second attack aimed at Stalingrad. As with the first campaign, German troops foundered in the Russian winter. The Soviet population endured tremendous sacrifices of property and lives to defeat the Germans. The victory, achieved at a cost of ten percent of the Russian population, was never forgotten.

C. The United States Enters the War

The United States' contribution to the war effort before 1941 was entirely economic. The United States considered Germany, not Japan, the primary enemy. U.S. relations with Japan suffered as a result of Japanese invasions in Thailand and Indochina. Nevertheless, when Japan successfully bombed the American Pacific fleet at Pearl Harbor on 7 December 1941, it came as a complete surprise. The U.S. declaration of war against Japan was followed by Hitler's declaration of war against the United States. Although the U.S. was militarily weak at the time of Pearl Harbor, the nation possessed vast industrial capacity and natural resources.

D. Winning the War in Europe

Strategy in a two-front war required that the Americans initiate some action in the Pacific against the Japanese to relieve the besieged forces of the British Empire and also open a second front in Europe to take some pressure off the Soviet Union. Although the Americans and British opened an offensive from Africa into the Mediterranean and Italy, it did little to alleviate the Russian dilemma. In 1943 Stalin, Churchill, and President Franklin Roosevelt met in Teheran to discuss opening another front in Europe. In June 1944, Britain and the United States invaded France at Normandy. Allied forces raced across northern France to Paris and on to the German border. Only briefly delayed by the German offensive at the Battle of the Bulge, the Allies crossed the Rhine in 1945. The Russian army entered Berlin and brought the European phase of the war to an end in April 1945.

E. Japanese War Aims and Assumptions

The Japanese promoted their efforts in World War II as an end to Western imperialism in Asia. The Greater East Asia Co-Prosperity Sphere, begun in 1940 to link all peoples and economies of the Pacific and Asia under Japanese domination, soon deteriorated into a new form of imperialism, with Japan as the colonial power. Japan viewed Southeast Asia as a market for Japanese manufactured goods and as a source of raw materials and food supplies. The Japanese regarded all other ethnic groups in Asia as their racial inferiors and required ritual obedience. The Chinese were regarded as culturally advanced, but their cultural sophistication did not prevent their wholesale destruction at the hands of Japanese troops. With respect to Westerners, the Japanese insisted on their own moral superiority. Purification consisted of requiring the Japanese population to endure wartime scarcity and material poverty. The moral inferiority of Westerners was reflected in their desire for grisly trophies of war. Because they viewed Europeans and Americans as morally deficient, the Japanese did not believe they could mobilize for long-term warfare. Their assessment proved inaccurate.

160

F. Winning the War in the Pacific

In the Pacific, American forces hopped from island to island, driving out the Japanese. American naval forces won the critical battle of the Pacific war at Midway, where the Japanese carrier forces were decimated. By 1945 the United States had obtained bases sufficiently close to Japan to initiate heavy bombing of the Japanese homeland. The air assault culminated in the atomic bombing of Hiroshima and Nagasaki. The Japanese government surrendered in September 1945.

G. The Fate of Allied Cooperation: 1945

Fifty million people died during the Second World War, most of them civilians. War was intentionally extended to noncombatants as a questionable means of destroying the will of civilian populations to resist. Material devastation of cities and industry was almost total. Europe and Japan were crippled; only the United States survived unscathed. The leaders of the victorious nations plotted the postwar world even before the final battles. The governments of Germany and Japan were to be utterly destroyed. New governments were to be established under the direct authority of the Allies. Stalin decided that the eastern European nations, invaded in 1945, had to remain subject to Russian domination as a means of guaranteeing the security of the Soviet Union.

TIMELINE

Insert the following events into the timeline. This should help you to compare important historical events chronologically.

Munich Conference held   Germany attacks Poland, initiates World War II
Japan Invades China   Allied forces land in Normandy
Japan attacks Pearl Harbor   Churchill, Roosevelt, Stalin meet at Teheran

1937	
1938	
1939	
1941	
1943	
1944	

TERMS, PEOPLE, EVENTS

The following terms, people, and events are important to your understanding of the chapter. Define each one.

Axis   atom bomb   Big Three
Grand Alliance   Neville Chamberlain   Munich Conference
Appeasement   Pact of Steel   Non-Aggression Pact of 1939
phony war   Battle of Britain   Winston Churchill
Blitzkrieg   Vichy   Charles de Gaulle
Collaborators   Josip Broz (Tito)   Final Solution
Zyklon B   Auschwitz   Warsaw ghetto
Stalingrad   Great Patriotic War   Tripartite Pact
Pearl Harbor   Teheran Conference   Yalta Conference
Potsdam Conference   Douglas MacArthur   Greater East Asia Co-Prosperity Sphere
Chester Nimitz   Midway   Hiroshima
Nagasaki

MAP EXERCISE

The following exercise is intended to clarify the geophysical environment and the spatial relationships among the important objects and places mentioned in the chapter.

1. In what ways did the expansion of Germany and Japan during World War II reflect their prewar concerns with imperialism? How did the expansion reflect the failure of treaty provisions after World War I?

2. Locate the following places on the map.

    Identify the nations included in the Greater East Asia Co-Prosperity Sphere.
    Identify the nations controlled by or allied with Germany.

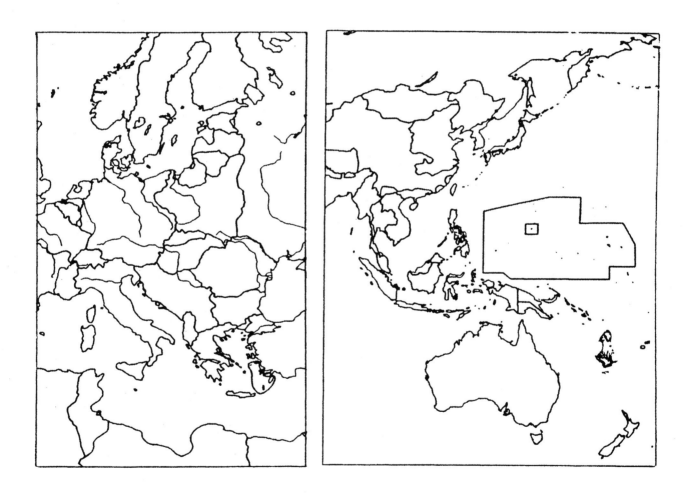

MAKING CONNECTIONS

The following questions are intended to emphasize important ideas within the chapter.

1. What was the goal of Hitler's foreign policy before 1939? What was the policy of appeasement? Why was it necessary?

2. How did the first stage of World War II in Europe go? How did Hitler's forces sweep across Europe so swiftly?

3. At whom were Hitler's policies of racial purity directed? What was the "Final Solution"? How was it enforced? Why did the Allies not take steps to halt the destruction of Europe's Jews?

4. What was the Great Patriotic War? Why was it so critical to Allied victory in World War II? What was its outcome?

5. Why did the United States enter World War II? What agreements between the Allies were necessary in order to win the war in Europe?

6. What was the Greater East Asia Co-Prosperity Sphere? In what sense were Japan's racial attitudes similar to those of Hitler?

7. What were the decisions reached at the series of conferences held by the leaders of the Allied powers? Why did the Soviet Union determine that its security required control of eastern Europe?

PUTTING LARGER CONCEPTS TOGETHER

The following questions test your ability to summarize the major conclusions of the chapter.

1. What were the war aims of Japan and Germany? How are these war aims related to the events from 1920 to 1939 in Europe and Asia?

2. What factors led to the defeat of the Axis powers? If you were asked the question, "What nation contributed most to the Allied victory?" how would you answer? Compare the relative contributions of the European powers to those of the Soviet Union and the United States.

SELF-TEST OF FACTUAL INFORMATION

1. Prior to World War II, with what nation did Hitler believe war was inevitable?

    a. Britain
    b. France
    c. the Soviet Union
    d. the United States

2. What was the primary objective of Hitler's assault on Czechoslovakia?

    a. to protect Germans living in Czechoslovakia
    b. to provoke a war with Britain
    c. to flank the French Maginot line
    d. to remove the greatest obstacle to an attack on living space farther east

3. The policy adopted by France and England to concede to Hitler's demand was called

    a. detente.
    b. rapprochement.
    c. appeasement.
    d. utilitarianism.

4. Which of the following statements concerning Nazi racial policies is MOST accurate?

    a. The Nazis only targeted Jews in their quest for racial purity.
    b. The Nazis concentrated their discrimination against lesbian women.
    c. Hitler's policies for the extermination of the Jews were already in place before 1938.
    d. Mass racial extermination actually began with the conquest of Poland.

5. Which of the following statements concerning the Holocaust is MOST accurate?

    a. Much of the blame for the Holocaust rests with the Jews themselves, who failed to resist the Germans.
    b. Most countries softened the effects of the Holocaust by admitting Jewish refugees throughout the war.
    c. Although their existence was never publicly announced, the concentration camps were known to many German citizens during the war.
    d. The United States actively bombed the concentration camps to bring the mass executions to a halt.

6. Hitler's defeat after 1941 hinged on which of the following?

    a. Britain's massive armies
    b. the success of resistance groups
    c. Soviet fighting power
    d. France's Vichy government

7. What event caused the United States to enter World War II?

    a. the Japanese attack on Pearl Harbor
    b. the German assault on Stalingrad
    c. the Italian invasion of Ethiopia
    d. Britain's appeal for help in the Battle of Britain

8. In what area was the second front initially opened in the European theater of World War II?

    a. Normandy
    b. the Mediterranean
    c. Gallipoli
    d. Finland

9. The Greater East Asia Co-Prosperity Sphere

    a. coordinated resistance to the Japanese advance.
    b. represented the first alliance in Asian history to recognize the total equality of all members.
    c. subordinated the rest of Asia to the economic needs of Japan.
    d. resulted in broad economic gains for all members.

10. In the series of conferences between 1943 and 1945, the Big Three

    a. agreed not to dismantle the governments of Japan and Germany.
    b. discussed the terms for a negotiated surrender of Germany and Japan.
    c. agreed to dismember Germany among themselves.
    d. described eastern Europe as an open zone with no attachments to any of the Allies.

CHAPTER 29

Postwar Recovery and the New Europe 1945-1970

OUTLINE

I.   Europe in Ruins

After the war, Europe was in ruins. Its cities were piles of rubble, there were millions of homeless refugees and the economies had collapsed.

II.   The Origins of the Cold War

A. Introduction

The Second World War left Europe in ruins. The United States and the Soviet Union had different concepts of postwar Europe. Their differences resulted in the Cold War.

B. The World in Two Blocks

The Second World War left the U.S. and the Soviet Union as the two strongest powers. Three decades of distrust and ideological differences quickly turned them into foes. Germany and Berlin were to be administered by the four Allied powers. By 1948 cooperation failed and Germany was divided into a western zone under the direction of the U.S., Britain, and France and a Soviet-dominated zone in the east. In order to protest the economic reconstruction of western Germany, the USSR blockaded the western districts of Berlin in 1948. The Russian blockade was halted when an American airlift of goods relieved the Berlin population. In 1949 the division of Germany into two separate governments—the western Federal Republic of Germany and the eastern German Democratic Republic—became permanent. Germany's division was symptomatic of the separation on the entire world into two, ideologically opposite, camps. All of Eastern Europe fell into the orbit of the Soviet Union.

The U.S. initiated a policy of containing the Soviet Union and created alliances to surround its enemy. The United States formed NATO in Europe, SEATO in Southeast Asia, and CENTO in the Middle East. To balance the U.S. alliances, the Soviet Union formed the Warsaw Pact that brought together all of the Eastern European nations dominated by the USSR.

C. The Nuclear Club

At the end of the Second World War only the United States had nuclear technology at its disposal, In 1949, the Soviet Union developed its own nuclear bomb and by 1974 Britain, France, India and China had also joined the Nuclear club. The proliferation of nuclear weapons produced paranoia among the political leadership of each superpower as they raced to dedicate more national resources to the development of more powerful weapons.

Despite arms limitations agreements to limit the testing and spread of nuclear weapons continued.

D. Decolonization

The end of World War II brought an end to the empires of western Europe. In India Mahatma Gandhi led a campaign of passive resistance against British rule that led to self-government in 1946. Pakistan and India separated into Muslim and Hindu states. The British colonies of Burma and Ceylon similarly achieved independence in 1948.

The Japanese empire dissolved in the aftermath of World War II. Independence movements in Asia tended to be communist. Communists came to power in China in 1949. Korea was divided at the end of the Second World War. Communist China supported North Korea in a war to annex South Korea, an ally of the United States. After three years of war, Korea was permanently divided in 1953. In Indochina communist insurgents waged war against the French until 1954, at which time Vietnam was divided into a communist state in the North under Ho Chi Minh and a South Vietnamese state protected by the United States. The Communists continued to press for independence until 1973, when the United States withdrew its forces from the south.

In Africa decolonization occurred in the 1950s and 1960s. By 1960 Britain and Belgium were prepared to grant independence to their colonies. Of the British colonies only Rhodesia and South Africa retained ruling white minorities. The French resisted relinquishing their colonies. In Algeria a war for independence dragged on from 1954-1962 and brought France to the brink of political collapse. In 1962, General Charles de Gaulle, agreed to grant Algeria independence. Despite independence, former colonies continued to be dominated by the industrialized powers of the West.

In the Middle East, both the Soviet Union and the United States used their economic aid to create friendly states. The U.S. gave its support of the new state of Israel while Egypt and Syria turned to the Soviet Union for aid. The oil-rich regions of Iran were also a bone of contention between the superpowers. To prevent the growth of Soviet influence, the U.S. assassinated a political leader in Iran and put a puppet government in place. In 1956 Egypt nationalized the Suez Canal. When the British and French attempt to regain control of the canal, joint pressure by the U.S. and the Soviet Union forced them to withdraw. The creation of Israel at the expense of Palestinian nationalist interests produced instability in the region.

The U. S. also acted to prevent the spread of communism in Latin America, often without success. Heavy-handed U.S. policies caused anti-Americanism in Latin American countries. In 1959 Fidel Castro led a successful communist revolution in Cuba. By 1962 the USSR and the U.S. were threatening war over the existence of missiles in Cuba. The crisis passed when Khrushchev ordered the dismantling of the missile bases.

III.   Postwar Economic Recovery in Europe, Japan and the Soviet Union

A. Introduction

In contrast to the Soviet Union with its destroyed cities and economy ravaged by war, the United States emerged from World War II economically prosperous and looking for new markets.

B. The Economic Challenge

The war reduced the European population and destroyed the physical plants of its industries. The war created millions of displaced persons who needed to be repatriated. Housing even the reduced European population was impossible. Agricultural production was at fifty percent of prewar levels. Without internal sources of investment capital to rebuild, Europe was dependent on money from abroad.

C. The Economic Solution: The Marshall Plan

In the aftermath of World War II, the U.S. sought to establish new markets, particularly in light of the collapse of the productive capacity of Western European industries. In both Europe and Japan, the United States acted to restore economies as potential consumers of American goods. The Truman Doctrine stated the principle that American aid would be forthcoming to nations resistant to Communism. More concretely the U.S. initiated the Marshall Plan to reconstruct Europe. Most Western European nations eagerly accepted the U.S. offer of aid. The Soviet Union and the Eastern European states refused, despite being eligible under the initial terms of the plan. The Marshall Plan did achieve the economic resuscitation of Western Europe without producing massive inflation.

D. Western European Economic Integration

With the Marshall Plan came the tendency toward state control on national economies. On the economic models of John Maynard Keynes, states targeted full employment and were active in spending to initiate capital formation. The Office of European Economic Cooperation, the mechanism for administering the Marshall Plan, coordinated state planning and creation of international trade networks. The Marshall Plan began the process of economic integration in Europe. Integration of Europe was furthered by the Council of Europe which served as a forum for discussing questions of common concern. The first supranational economic union was Benelux—an economic alliance of Belgium, the Netherlands, and Luxembourg. By 1951 the Benelux nations along with France, Italy, and West Germany formed the European Coal and Steel Community that established a common market for coal and steel among member countries. The same countries created the European Economic Community, also known as the Common Market, in 1957 for the purpose of extending the integration of all markets. Great Britain joined the EEC in 1973. By the nature of its membership, the EEC sharpened economic and political differences between Eastern and Western Europe.

169

E. Japan's Recovery

Under military occupation, Japan also received U.S. economic aid. With the support of the U.S., the Japanese economy rapidly modernized its destroyed physical plant. Without a military budget (the military was abolished after the war), capital could be directed entirely to industrial development. By the 1960s, Japan was an industrial giant with an affluent consumer society.

F. Soviet Path to Economic Recovery

The Soviet Union countered the Marshal Plan with Comecon to promote economic reconstruction and to integrate the East European economies for the benefit of the Soviet Union. Under Stalin's leadership Soviet Industry recovered making the Soviet Union the second largest industrial power. The Soviet domination of Eastern Europe was altered by Stalin's death in 1953 and his replacement by Nikita Khrushchev. Khrushchev's denunciation of Stalin gave the impression that reform was imminent. Nationalist Communist leaders emerged in Poland and Hungary. The tempted liberalization in Hungary was suppressed by the Russian army. Soviet standard of living remained low as, all economic gain was plowed back into heavy industry. Despite Khrushchev's promises of reform, the Soviet economy could not sustain increases in consumable items and a massive expenditure for a growing atomic arsenal. The Eastern European nations aligned with the USSR adopted Russian strategies for development of heavy industries with similar results: industrialization advanced but standards of living did not. To prevent immigration from Eastern Europe to the West through Berlin, the USSR constructed a wall in 1961 that symbolized the separation of political ideologies. In 1968 the liberal Czechoslovakian government of Alexander Dubcek was overthrown. Only Tito in Yugoslavia retained his independence.

III.   The Welfare State & Social Transformation

A. Introduction

In the aftermath of the Second World War, states formed welfare programs to provide for the support of their citizens, particularly children and the family. Countries attempted to resolve the issues of birth, sickness, old age, and unemployment.

B. Prosperity and Consumption in the West

The postwar recovery of Europe produced greater per capita wealth. The creation of welfare programs insured the safety of that wealth from disastrous economic consequences. As a result, people felt less restraint in spending. The new consumer economy did not redistribute wealth. The rich got richer and the poor stayed dependent on welfare. Women remained far behind in terms of pay for work.

170

C. Family Strategies

Unlike the U.S., there was only a temporary surge in the birth rate in Europe following the Second World War. More forms of birth control became readily available by the 1960s, and women chose to have smaller families. In contrast, men and women desperately sought to reestablish family life after the war. In Britain women were once again urged to take up their accustomed place in the domestic household. Women were discouraged from joining the workforce, sometimes by justifying lower pay as an economic disincentive. The welfare system generally reinforced the financial dependence of women on men. In France women were accepted in the workforce and achieved literal equality with men in the welfare state. During the 1960s protests against government policies—civil rights and freedom of expression—became more common. Women's equality was one of the issues most hotly debated. Simone de Beauvoir's *The Second Sex* (1949) urged women to define sexuality and gender relationships in their own terms. The movement for women's rights continued to grow into the 1970s.

D. Youth Culture and Dissent

The social tension created by the threat of nuclear war and growing economic affluence created a generation of dissenters. Young men and women rejected the cultural traditions of their parents and experimented with sexual freedom, drugs, and political radicalism. Birth control removed one of the major constraints to freer sexuality. Sex for pleasure outside the family unit became an acceptable form of social expression within the youth movement. Women were often exploited as sexual objects in films and magazines. The use of drugs expanded beyond medical purposes to production of experiences ranging from hedonistic gratification to mind-altering hallucination. Drugs allowed affluent young people to escape the limits of their society and flout the values of their elders.

By 1969 political protests were common in the U.S. and in western Europe. Protests in the 1960s coalesced around opposition to the war in Vietnam. Student protests, sometimes involving occupation of university buildings, were occasionally met with police repression. Most of the young protesters were members of the middle class. In Europe the mood of protest was exacerbated by a slowing economy that no longer offered guarantees of economic security. In 1969 a French protest spread beyond the University of Paris to the surrounding city, then the entire country. For a brief moment the working class and the bourgeois students were united in rejecting the political programs of the government. The moment quickly passed, because the two groups had so little in common.

TIMELINE

Insert the following events into the timeline. This should help you to compare important historical events chronologically.

Marshall Plan initiated   The Berlin Wall built
death of Stalin   formation of EEC
The Second Sex published   Wave of Protests at European Universities

1947	
1949	
1953	
1957	
1961	
1968	

TERMS, PEOPLE, EVENTS

The following terms, people, and events are important to your understanding of the chapter. Define each one.

Marshall Plan   John Maynard Keynes   Wladlislaw Gomulka
Common Market   Nikita Khrushchev   decolonization
welfare state   women's liberation   Free Speech movement
Charles de Gaulle   Simone de Beauvoir   Iron Curtain
De-Stalinization   Comecon   Protonatalism
Cold War   Cntainment   Third World
NATO   Nuclear Club   Prague Spring

MAP EXERCISE

The following exercise is intended to clarify the geophysical environment and the spatial relationships among the important objects and places mentioned in the chapter.

1. How did participation in the Marshall Plan match the diplomatic division of Europe between the United States and the Soviet Union? How did participation in the plan foreshadow the growth of European economic integration? Why?

2. Locate the following places on the map:

    Identify the states associated with the United States through the Marshal Plan
    The 6 countries that were the original members of the EEC in 1957
    Identify the States associated with the Warsaw Pact

MAKING CONNECTIONS

The following questions are intended to emphasize important ideas within the chapter.

1. What were the causes of the Cold War? How did the superpowers attempt to divide and control Europe?

2. How was the rest of the world affected by the political bipolarity of postwar Europe?

3. What was the economic situation of Europe after World War II and how was it resolved? How did the economic resolution differ in Eastern and Western Europe?

4. Define welfare state. How did the welfare state define social progress?

5. What were the causes of the "generation gap" that emerged in the 1960s?

PUTTING LARGER CONCEPTS TOGETHER

The following question tests your ability to summarize the major conclusions of the chapter.

1. How was the economic structure of Europe after World War II different from the period before 1939? Consider the role of the state in economic policy and social welfare. How different were the policies of Eastern and western Europe?

SELF-TEST OF FACTUAL INFORMATION

1. The first nuclear test-ban treaty was signed in

    a. 1956.
    b. 1962.
    c. 1963.
    d. 1968.

2. All of the following were alliances created by the United States to contain Soviet Expansion EXCEPT

    a. NATO
    b. the Bagdad Pact.
    c. The Comecon
    d. SEATO.

3. Agricultural productivity in 1945 had fallen to what percentage of prewar capacity?

    a. 20
    b. 30
    c. 40
    d. 50

4. The United States' program of economic relief to Europe after World War II was called the

    a. Sykes-Picot Agreement.
    b. Marshall Plan.
    c. Balfour Plan.
    d. Dulles Initiative.

5. Keynesian economics argued for all the following EXCEPT

    a. "laissez faire" government policies.
    b. full employment.
    c. elimination of boom-and-bust cycles.
    d. "priming the pump."

6. All of the following statements concerning the postwar Soviet economy are true EXCEPT that

   a. the standard of living remained low.
   b. per capita productivity remained low.
   c. defense spending consumed a large amount of the economy.
   d. Soviet and Eastern bloc women received pay equal to males.

7. The man who led the movement for Indian Independence

   a. Patrice Lumunba
   b. Mahatma Gandhi
   c. Jomo Kenyata.
   d. Abdel Nassar.

8. What Soviet leader was the first to denounce the policies of Joseph Stalin in the 1950s?

   a. Mikhail Gorbachev
   b. Yuri Andropov
   c. Boris Yeltsin
   d. Nikita Khmshchev

9. What was a welfare state?

   a. states in which the entire population required government assistance
   b. states with social programs intended to provide security from the challenges of birth, sickness, and unemployment
   c. states that guaranteed equality to everyone, regardless of sex or age
   d. states that insisted on free-market economics and generally left social programs up to local communities

10. A handbook for the women's protest movement after 1945 was

    a. *Animal Farm.*
    b. *The Second Sex.*
    c. *Future Shock.*
    d. *Atlas Shrugged.*

CHAPTER 30

The End of the Cold War and New Global Challenges, 1970 to the Present

OUTLINE

I.   The Berlin Wall Comes Down

In 1961 the East German Government built the Berlin War to keep East Germans from migrating to West Germany in search of a better standard of living. For 28 years the 90 mile wall served as a symbol of the ideological divisions of the Cold War. In November of 1989 the East German Government ended restrictions of travel between East and West and the wall was taken down. Its fall symbolized the end of the Cold War.

II. The End of the Cold War and The Emergence of a new Europe

A. Introduction

From 1945 to the 1980s the Cold War ordered the world into two-opposing blocks. At the same time it preserved an uneasy peace between the superpowers. Beginning in the mid-1960s, growing discontent among citizens of the Soviet block began to show stresses in the Communist regimes.

B. The Brezhnev Doctrine and Détente

Soviet leader Leonid Brezhnev (1966-1982) declared the right of the Soviet Union to intervene in the internal affairs of the members of the Warsaw Pact in order to suppress counterrevolution. During the 1970s the confrontational nature of diplomatic relationships between the USSR and the U.S. was replaced by a spirit of cooperation called detente. Nuclear weapons limitation treaties were negotiated and signed. During the 1980s, there was a temporary return to the Cold War. President Ronald Reagan of the U.S. revived the traditional enmity between the superpowers. Reagan attempted to restart the arms race by seeking to place weapons in space. Despite Reagan's militancy, Cold War tensions generally lessened.

C. New Direction in Soviet Politics

By the 1980s it was clear that the Brezhnev doctrine had failed to end dissent within the Soviet Block. In the Soviet Union there also was growing dissent especially among leading intellectuals. One of the leading dissidents was Andrei Sakharov who along with other intellectual dissidents produced literature, censored by the government, that revealed the abuses of the Soviet government. For his pains, Sakharov was exiled in the closed city of Gorki until 1986 when the former nuclear scientist was rehabilitated during the government of Mikhail Gorbachev.

With the accession of Mikhail Gorbachev in 1985 the atmosphere of repression in the Soviet Union lightened. Gorbachev attempted to address the relatively low standard of living endured by Soviet citizens. While workers had money to spend, there were virtually no better-quality goods available for consumption. Unfortunately, Gorbachev was unable to increase sufficiently the production of consumer goods. Soviet citizens turned to the black market to purchase products from the U.S. and western Europe. Gorbachev responded by creating a limited free market and lessening restrictions on importation of Western goods. Gorbachev also attempted to limit military expenditures in the hope of increasing investment in consumer goods.

D. Reform in Eastern Europe

Gorbachev's reforms in the Soviet Union opened the possibility of change in eastern Europe. Polish resistance to Soviet rule was centered in the industrial city of Gdansk. To forestall price rises of food and necessities, the Polish government depended on foreign loans in the 1970s. When the government could no longer borrow, it ordered price increases in 1976 that were soon rescinded in the face of strikes. When prices were again raised in 1980, the shipyard workers of Gdansk under the leadership of Lech Walesa formed a non-Communist union, Solidarity, and shut down the shipyards. The union's success in forcing government reforms gave it political power. In 1981 the government attempted to use the military to crack down on labor dissidents, but the Soviet Union refused to add its military power. Solidarity was finally legalized in 1989. In elections held in that year, Solidarity candidates swept the Communist party out of office. Solidarity faced the same economic problems that had baffled their Communist predecessors. In the 1990s Poland pursued free market policies by attracting western companies to open subsidiaries in Poland. In 1989 Hungary opened all its borders to the West and immigrants poured into western Europe. The Communist government in Hungary was replaced by a new socialist regime. Student protests that mushroomed into a mass democratic movement initiated the political change in Czechoslovakia. Like its Hungarian neighbor, the Czech Communist government was voted out of power and replaced by the democratic opposition led by Vaclav Havel. Only in Romania did revolutionaries violently overthrow the government of Nicolae Ceaucescu. After the government ordered the military to fire on protestors, a popular revolution seized the former ruler and executed him in 1989.

E. The Unification of Germany

East Germany and West Germany developed as two separate countries and societies in the 1960s and 1970s. However, economically they were virtually a single economy by 1980. When West Germany joined the EEC in 1957, it required that East and West Germany be treated as a single nation for purposes of trade. West Germany established important trade markets in its eastern neighbor. Economic linkage led to cultural identity. The major problem caused by the economic relationship between East and West Germany was the tendency of skilled laborers and professionals to leave the East in search of higher salaries and better living conditions in the West. Emigration became a flood by the late 1980s. In 1989 the East German government was forced to remove the

Berlin Wall and open its borders. Within a year political unification of East and West Germany was accomplished. The new nation faced immediate problems. Other European nations were wary of a reunited Germany. The former East Germans were concerned about marginalization and economic subservience within the new nation.

F.   Russia and the New Republics

Gorbachev's rhetoric of reform brought forth grass-roots political movements dedicated to reducing the role of the Communist party. In 1990 Gorbachev ended the political monopoly of the Communist party in the Soviet Union. Criticism of Gorbachev's unwillingness to embark on even more radical reforms grew. In August 1991 Communist party conservatives attempted to seize power and overthrow the Gorbachev government. Although the coup failed, Gorbachev's political prestige was fatally damaged. Boris Yeltsin replaced Gorbachev as the most influential politician in Russian politics. Gorbachev's attempt to open the Russian economy to greater market influence foundered on the combined problems of an insecure currency and the development of the Russian mafia. Despite economic struggles, the greatest threat to Gorbachev's more open system was the "nationalities problem," the existence of ethnic minorities, in the USSR. There were three major areas of nationalism within the Soviet Union: Central Asia, Armenia, and the Baltic states. In Latvia, Lithuania, and Estonia, ethnic minorities demanded nationalist self-determination instead of Communist party solidarity. Violence broke out in Armenia between groups of ethnic Azerbaijanis and Armenians. Soviet troops were sent to the area. Rioting in Central Asia was instigated by university students. By 1991 all fifteen Soviet republics declared their independence from the Soviet Union. Gorbachev resigned as head of the Soviet Union on 25 December 1991, and Boris Yeltsin became the leading political figure of Russia. Eleven republics formed the Commonwealth of Independent States. Control of the Soviet military and serious economic problems remained unresolved as a new constitution was created for Russia in 1993, but political instability continued to exist. An uneasy alliance of former communists and radical nationalists challenged Yeltsin for control of the new nation. He withstood the challenge and was elected to a second term in 1996.

III.   Ethnic Conflict and Nationalism

A. Introduction

The collapse of communism unleashed a wave of violence, terrorism and ethnic cleansing over long-standing grievances.

B. The Chechen Challenge

In 1994 Boris Yeltsin committed Russia's military forces to suppress a nationalist rebellion in the province of Chechnya. Attacks on civilian targets roused international opposition to the conflict. Although he promised an end to the war in his political campaign of 1996, Yeltsin was slow to begin a withdrawal of Russian forces from Chechnya. Although a truce was declared, Yeltsin's disappearance from political events

179

seemed to signal insecurity at the top of the Russian government. In 1999 Chechen terrorism in Moscow led to renewed war to suppress the Chechen revolutionaries. In 2001 Russian president Vladimir Putin declared the war over, but the violence continued to escalate between Russian and Chechnyan fighters. The continuing Russian occupation pushed the Chechnyans to turn to terrorism against Russian civilians, including the killing of 339 hostages at a school. President Putin responded by curtailing democracy.

B. War in the Balkans

Of all the former Communist states, Yugoslavia had appeared most free of Soviet influence and closer to economic integration in the western European economy. By 1991, however, Yugoslavia, disintegrated into competing ethnic groups, attempted to restore ethnic homogeneity in regions of the former Yugoslav state.

Dating back to the outset of the twentieth century, there were hostilities among the various ethnic groups in the Balkans. Serbs, typically Orthodox, and Croats, typically Catholic, were traditionally opposed to each other. Conflicting territorial claims of the two groups were complicated by the existence of a sizable minority of Muslims living in the disputed territory of Bosnia. Beginning in 1992, the Serbs attempted to seize the territory of Bosnia as part of a "greater Serbia," and began a policy of "ethnic cleansing" of Muslims living in the region. Muslim volunteers from outside of Bosnia supported Muslim defenses. In 1995 NATO intervened in the conflict to halt the Serbian advance. Eventually the Dayton Peace Accord halted conflict. Despite the peace, ethnic differences continued to exist, and the nation remained divided.

In 1998 conflict broke out over Kosovo, a portion of Serbia with a large Albanian ethnic minority. Ethnic Albanians desired to break away from Serbia and unite with Albania and Macedonia to form a new nation in the Balkans. The Serb government began a calculated plan to force the emigration of ethnic Albanians from Kosovo. In 1999 NATO forces intervened to halt the "ethnic cleansing" of Kosovo. When the Serb forces withdrew, Albanians returned to Kosovo and began to drive out Serbs from the region. All of the Balkans continued to experience weak economies. But Albania was in the worst economic shape. With the collapse of communism, Albania disintegrated into a primitive society plagued by banditry.

IV.   The West in the Global Community

A. Introduction

Western economies, fueled by a growing supply of cheap labor from southern Europe and former colonies, continued to grow until the oil crisis of the 1970s. During the 1970s and 1980s, the expense of the welfare state prompted political reevaluations. Economic integration in the Common Market continued to reflect the Western European trend to a single market and unified economic policies.

B. European Union and the American Superpower

The founders of the European Economic Community (EEC) intended the creation of a united Europe; but until the oil crisis of the 1970s abated, the EEC had little power over its individual national governments. In order to compete against Japan and the U.S. for foreign markets, greater economic integration was desirable. In 1985 the Single European Act was drafted and accepted by all member states. It was intended to establish a single, integrated European market by the end of 1992. The act, removed all tariff barriers and effective frontiers to limit movement or trade. At Maastricht in 1991, the various governments approved the Treaty on the European Union, but there remained doubts about the ability of the various nations to create a single European state. In the 1990s Europe began to move to a unified defense system, common social and economic policies and in 2002 adopted a single currency called the euro. By 2004 there were 25 member states in the European union including several from eastern Europe. The potential of a unified European economy caused concern in trading rivals, including the United States and Japan. Nevertheless, by the end of the 1990s, the United States was embarking on a closer economic relationship with the European union as American companies entered into partnerships and joint ventures with European companies.

C. A New Working Class: Foreign Workers

Industrial growth in Western European nations depended on ready supplies of cheap, unskilled labor. Southern Europe, Asia, the Caribbean, and Africa supplied immigrants to fill the labor pool. Most migrants were males without families, who intended to make their fortunes and return to their homelands. In most cases they did not. Foreign laborers—men and women—endured harsh living conditions in keeping with the low prestige associated with their menial labor. Cultural acceptance proved impossible, even after several generations in the adopted country. Poor relations between immigrants and natives led to violence. Right-wing politicians in western Europe demanded limitations on immigration and portrayed foreign workers as threats to domestic workers. Racial rioting directed against communities of foreign workers broke out in France and Great Britain. In response to the flood of immigration and growing opposition to foreigners in the workforce, most countries enacted restrictions against foreign immigration after 1973 and the oil crisis. Even non-European political refugees were refused entry into some countries. France halted immigration entirely in 1974. In general, the restrictions failed to diminish the numbers of foreign workers in western Europe. By the 1990s immigration had become a major issue in electoral campaigns that allowed extreme right wing politicians to become prominent. The presence of large numbers of foreign workers resulted in a cultural clash. In 2004 France enforced cultural uniformity by prohibiting the wearing of clothing in school that denoted religious affiliation.

D Women's Changing Lives

Western women were more educated and had access to more professional positions in the last quarter of the twentieth century. Feminist scholarship incorporated women's issues into school and university curricula. Parallel to the increase of economic and educational

181

opportunities for women was the development of an international women's movement. Women's political action led to changes. Italian women gained the limited right to divorce their husbands in 1970; French women gained access to legalized abortion in 1975. Radical feminists urged separatism—a war between the sexes, because they saw women as an oppressed sex. Feminists in the 1970s and 1980s adopted a number of related political issues such as peace and nuclear weapons, and in the 1990s they also became prominent in the environmental issues. The women's movement also affected social relationships in the Soviet Union, but to a lesser extent. Like their Western counterparts, Soviet women were better educated at the end of the twentieth century. Eastern women actually enjoyed better representation in parliamentary bodies, but held virtually no offices with actual power within the Communist party. In the work force, Soviet women were numerous—often performing menial jobs—but held few managerial positions. Support mechanisms—child care, kindergartens, pre-natal care—were lacking in the Soviet Union. Birthrates in the Soviet Union continued to fall, as they did in western Europe.

E. Terrorism: The "New Kind of War"

Terrorism continued to be a significant means of political expression in the late twentieth century. The creation of the state of Israel in the Middle East and the loss of autonomy by Palestinian Arabs led to international terrorism. Palestinians, Islamic Fundamentalists and European supporters—the Red Army Faction of Germany and the Red Brigades of Italy—carried terrorism to the citizens of western Europe and the U.S. Terrorism was the heir of the European tradition of anarchism as a weapon of oppressed nationalist minorities. Victims were randomly chosen as symbols of oppression. Citizens of western Europe and the U.S. were important targets for terrorism, because their sacrifice offered the promise of media exposure of acts of violence. The U.S. status as the major power in the world made it a major terrorism target beginning in the 1980s. On September 11, 2001 a terrorist attack organized by Osama bin Laden destroyed the World Trade Center and part of the Pentagon leaving more than 3000 people dead. In the aftermath of the attack the U.S. and Great Britain invaded Afghanistan in what is called the "war on terrorism." Using the cover of the "war on terrorism" the United States invaded Iraq in March of 2003 and overthrew Saddam Hussein. Within months of the invasion the American occupation forces began to face resistance from insurgent fighters fighting American occupation. Terrorist groups represented all shades of the political spectrum from Marxists to right-wing nationalists, but formed cooperative networks of training bases and information. Terrorism was effective in gaining publicity for political causes and in disrupting western European society. Terrorists were able to avoid surveillance and detection. Yet despite the helplessness of the West in limiting acts of political violence, terrorists accomplished few concrete political goals. Western reactions to terrorism have varied from negotiation for the release of hostages to anti-terrorist military action. Israel and the U.S. have been most aggressive in striking back at identified terrorist groups. In 2004 it was revealed that the United States had resorted to torture and interrogation techniques that violated the Geneva Convention. Despite the tactic of meeting violence with violence the U.S. had not succeeded in ending its vulnerability to terrorism.

TIMELINE

Insert the following events into the timeline. This should help you to compare important historical events chronologically.

Solidarity established in Poland   Soviet Union dissolved
Berlin wall taken-down   United States invades Iraq
unification of two Germanys   NATO began attacks on Serbian positions in Kosovo

1980	
1989	
1990	
1991	
1999	
2004	

TERMS, PEOPLE, EVENTS

The following terms, people, and events are important to your understanding of the chapter. Define each one.

Boris Yeltsin	CIS	Détente
nationalities problem	Chechuya	Solidarity
Lech Walesa	Nicolae Ceaucescu	"velvet revolutions"
Vaclav Havel	Slobodan Milosevic	"greater Serbia"
Dayton Peace Accords	Kosovo	ethnic cleansing
MaastrichtTreaty	Single European Act	terrorism
migrant labor	EC	euro
Nagorno-Karabakh	Osama bin Laden	Vladimir Putin
Andrei Sakharov	*samizdat*	Mikhail Gorbachev
Leonid Brezhnev	Brezhnev Doctrine	Boris Yeltsin
Perestroika	glasnost	European Economic Community
Jihad	European Union	Nationalities problem

MAP EXERCISE

The following exercise is intended to clarify the geophysical environment and the spatial relationships among the important objects and places mentioned in the chapter.

1. One of the common themes of European history is the typical political fragmentation of central Europe. How does the political configuration of post-Soviet Europe conform to that theme? Is there any significant departure?

2. Locate the following places on the map.

   Identify all of the states created in the aftermath of the collapse of the Soviet Union.
   Identify new states in eastern Europe created out of former Yugoslavia and Czechoslovakia.

MAKING CONNECTIONS

The following questions are intended to emphasize important ideas within the chapter.

1. What was *détente*? How was it related to political changes in the Soviet Union and internal dissent?

2. What reforms did Mikhail Gorbachev attempt to impose on the Soviet Union? Consider political and economic reforms.

3. How did the nationalities problem contribute to the downfall of the Soviet Union? In what sense does the nationalities problem still trouble the internal politics of Russia?

4. What was Solidarity? How did the development of Solidarity affect the political regime of Poland? What factors permitted the "velvet revolutions?"

5. Why were nationality problems in the Balkans predictable?

6. What factors led to the reunification of East and West Germany? What potential threat did a reunited Germany pose to the rest of Europe?

7. How did large numbers of foreign workers, and terrorism affect the political development of western Europe? How did the feminist movement develop in the decades after 1970?

8. What were the stages in the creation of a unified European economy?

9. How has the problem of terrorism affected the western world since the early 1970s?

PUTTING LARGER CONCEPTS TOGETHER

The following questions test your ability to summarize the major conclusions of the chapter.

1. In what sense can it be said that the aftermath of the Cold War simply reproduced the normal state of political instability in Central Europe? Compare the current state of Europe with European political structure in 1650, 1750, and 1815.

2. How does the creation of increasingly democratic regimes in central Europe contrast with the development of economic centralization in western Europe? What potential conflicts are implied by these developments? How does the existence of a unified Germany highlight these difficulties?

SELF-TEST OF FACTUAL INFORMATION

1. In the Brezhnev Doctrine, the Soviet Union

    a. accepted the nuclear dominance of the United States and promised to lessen nuclear tension.
    b. promised to permit political deviation from Communism in nations of the Warsaw Pact.
    c. claimed the right to intervene in the internal affairs of the nations of the Warsaw Pact.
    d. offered to end the Cold War.

2. In 1994 Russia committed itself to war against which secessionist region?

    a. Chechnya
    b. Serbia
    c. Estonia
    d. Kazakhstan

3. Andrei Sakharov

    a. led the Soviet department charged with the economic rehabilitation of eastern Europe.
    b. wrote *The Gulag Archipelago*.
    c. was the leading Soviet dissident of the 1970s.
    d. led the coup that toppled Gorbachev from power in 1990.

4. Solidarity was a non-Communist union for

    a. farmers in Galicia.
    b. factory workers in Krackow.
    c. shipyard workers in Gdansk.
    d. party bureaucrats in Lodz.

5. When West Germany entered the European Union in 1957,

    a. East Germany was forbidden to ever become a member of the EU.
    b. Britain left the EU in protest.
    c. France launched an economic boycott of the German state.
    d. it insisted that the two Germanys be treated as a single political entity in terms of trade.

6.   Which of the following statements concerning the Balkan states is MOST accurate?

     a. Religious differences are not critical in the Balkans.
     b. Religious differences are limited to disputes between Catholic and Orthodox.
     c. The United States had maintained strict neutrality in the Balkan conflict.
     d. NATO, including the United States, has intervened militarily to end conflict.

7.   Which of the following nations was NOT one of the leading importers of unskilled labor
     after the 1950s?

     a. Great Britain
     b. France
     c. West Germany
     d. Italy

8.   Which of the following statements concerning Lech Walesa is NOT true?

     a. He received the Nobel Peace Prize in 1983.
     b. He was jailed during a period of martial law in Poland.
     c. He was the last Communist ruler of Poland prior to 1989.
     d. He was elected head of the Polish government after 1989.

9.   Ethnic violence became a problem in all the following EXCEPT

     a. Bosnia.
     b. Chechnya.
     c. Poland.
     d. Kosovo.

10. The European Community plan for economic integration in western Europe included all of
     the following EXCEPT

     a. a central banking system, the European Monetary Institute.
     b. a common currency.
     c. a common European defense system.
     d. the absolute exclusion of eastern European nations from the Community.

Answers to Chapter Self-Tests Or Factual Information

Chapter 14

l. d	6. c
2. b	7. b
3. c	8. d
4. b	9. b
5. c	10. c

Chapter 15

l. b	6. c
2. a	7. d
3. d	8. c
4. a	9. d
5. d	10. b

Chapter 16

l. a	6. a
2. c	7. b
3. d	8. b
4. c	9. a
5. b	10. d

Chapter 17

l. a	6. d
2. b	7. b
3. c	8. b
4. b	9. d
5. d	10. c

Chapter 18

l. b	6. c
2. b	7. b
3. c	8. b
4. c	9. d
5. a	10. b

Chapter 19

l. b	6. c
2. c	7. c
3. b	8. a
4. b	9. b
5. b	10. b

Chapter 20

l. d	6. c
2. a	7. d
3. c	8. a
4. b	9. a
5. a	10. c

Chapter 21

l. b	6. b
2. a	7. b
3. d	8. a
4. a	9. b
5. b	10. a

Chapter 22

l. c	6. b
2. b	7. d
3. d	8. b
4. c	9. b
5. b	10. c

Chapter 23

l. c	6. c
2. d	7. b
3. d	8. d
4. d	9. b
5. b	10. b

Chapter 24

l. d	6. c
2. d	7. c
3. d	8. a
4. c	9. a
5. a	10. a

Chapter 25

l. c	6. a
2. b	7. b
3. a	8. c
4. c	9. d
5. a	10. b

Chapter 26

l. b	6. b
2. a	7. d
3. c	8. b
4. b	9. b
5. c	10. c

Chapter 27

l. d	6. c
2. b	7. c
3. c	8. d
4. d	9. b
5. b	10. a

Chapter 28

l. c	6. c
2. d	7. a
3. c	8. b
4. d	9. c
5. c	10. c

Chapter 29

l. c	6. d
2. c	7. b
3. d	8. d
4. b	9. b
5. a	10. b

Chapter 30

l. c	6. d
2. a	7. d
3. c	8. c
4. c	9. d
5. d	10. d